RESPONSIBLE PARENTING NEWSLETTERS

Reproducible Newsletters for Parent Programs or Conferences

by

Robert Kline, Ph.D. & Julie E. Kline, M.A.

Reprinted 2001

copyright © 1998
mar⋆co products, inc.

Published by
mar⋆co products, inc.
1443 Old York Road
Warminster, PA 18974
1-800-448-2197

All rights reserved including the right of reproduction in whole or in part in any form. The purchaser may reproduce the activity sheets, free and without special permission, for student use for a particular group or class. Reproduction of these materials for distribution to any person other than the purchaser or an to entire school system is forbidden.

Library of Congress Catalog Card Number: 98-87797

ISBN: 1-57543-065-7

Printed in the U.S.A.

TABLE OF CONTENTS

INTRODUCTION 5

CHILDREN'S BEHAVIORS 7

    BED-WETTING 8
    COMING HOME ON TIME 9
    DAWDLING 10
    DEMANDS 11
    FEAR OF DARKNESS 12
    FIGHTING (PHYSICAL AND VERBAL) 13
    HYPERACTIVITY 14
    INTERRUPTIONS 15
    LEAVING TOYS OUT OF PLACE 16
    LYING 17
    NAIL-BITING 18
    NAME-CALLING 19
    NIGHTMARES 20
    PAIN 21
    POOR EATING HABITS 22
    SCREAMING 23
    STEALING 24
    STUTTERING 25
    TALKING BACK 26
    TARDINESS 27
    TATTLING 28
    TEMPER TANTRUMS 29
    UNDESIRABLE FRIENDS 30

PRE-ADOLESCENT AND ADOLESCENT BEHAVIORS 31

    DATING OR ASSOCIATING WITH UNDESIRABLE FRIENDS 32
    DEPRESSION 33
    DIETING 34
    DRESS AND GROOMING 35
    DRINKING AND DRUG ABUSE 36

PARENT BEHAVIORS 37

    APOLOGIES 38
    AVOIDING COAXING 39
    BLUFFING 40
    BRIBES 41
    DEVELOPING INTERNAL MOTIVATION 42
    DIFFUSING ANGER 43
    DISTRACTING A CHILD 44
    EAVESDROPPING 45
    ENCOURAGEMENT 46
    FEELINGS OF INFERIORITY 47
    GIVING CHILDREN POWER 48
    SPECIAL NEEDS CHILDREN 49
    LEAVING CHILDREN IN THE CARE OF ANOTHER PERSON 50
    PARENTS' SCREAMING 51
    SINGLE-PARENT DATING 52
    TEASING 53
    TIME OUT 54

ACADEMIC CONCERNS 55

    FEAR OF SCHOOL 56
    HOMEWORK 57
    NOTE-HOME PROGRAM 58

HOUSEHOLD CONCERNS 59

    ALLOWANCES 60
    BEDTIME 61
    CHILDREN OF DIVORCE 62
    CHORES 63
    GETTING UP ON TIME 64
    GOING TO THE HOSPITAL 65
    MUSIC PRACTICE 66
    NEW BABY IN THE FAMILY 67
    ROOM-CLEANING 68
    VISITING THE DOCTOR 69
    WORKING PARENTS 70

ABOUT THE AUTHORS 72

INTRODUCTION

These newsletters are intended for parents. The behaviors have been presented to us repeatedly over the years. As this occurred, we found ourselves giving the same basic advice on each behavior. Our conclusion was that, in most cases, the misbehaving child did not need therapy. Rather, the family members just needed to know what to do, and they needed to have that information presented in a style they could understand and a format they could use.

In working with school personnel, we realized they were often asked by parents for help on the same topics. By using the newsletters available in this book, school personnel can offer assistance to parents when questions arise and also educate parents even if there is no specific request.

These newsletters are short and to-the-point. Therefore, parents are not faced with an overwhelming amount of reading matter.

Select the newsletters that interest you. Fill in your name or the name of your school after the "From" at the top of the page, and reproduce the copies you need. Then, make them available to your intended audience. You may choose to give them to individuals, pass them out during parent conferences, pass them out during parenting workshops, leave them in an appropriate place in the school office, or give them to teachers to pass out at parent conferences. Whatever your choice, you will be providing parents with an invaluable resource.

Robert Kline & Julie Kline

CHILDREN'S BEHAVIORS

This section includes 23 reproducible newsletters for parents concerning various behaviors of children from preschool to preadolescence featuring the following topics:

Bed-Wetting
Coming Home on Time
Dawdling
Demands
Fear of Darkness
Fighting (Physical and Verbal)
Hyperactivity
Interruptions
Leaving Toys Out of Place
Lying
Nail-Biting
Name-Calling/Being Picked On
Nightmares
Pain
Poor Eating Habits
Screaming
Stealing
Stuttering
Talking Back
Tardiness
Tattling
Temper Tantrums
Undesirable Friends

BED-WETTING

Don't let bed-wetting become an emotional issue. Treat it in a matter-of-fact way.

Bed-wetting, or enuresis, is fairly common with children under the age of five, and isn't really uncommon in children as old as six or seven. It is more of a nuisance to the parents than a problem for the child. After the age of seven, however, bed-wetting is likely to be associated with emotional problems and professional help should be considered. Before beginning any treatment, the child should have a physical examination to rule out infection or some other medical cause of the problem.

MEDICATION

Medications such as Imipramine or DDAVP spray, prescribed by pediatricians, are probably the most common approach to treatment. These medications have been widely used in the medical community. They don't work all the time, but they are effective in a fair number of cases. A common practice is to discontinue the medications for three weeks every six months to determine whether they are still necessary.

BUZZERS

Another way to treat bed-wetting is to buy a buzzer apparatus. When a child wets the bed, the buzzer sounds and awakens the child. This too, has had a fair amount of success. Be sure to use the device for two weeks after the child has stopped wetting the bed.

HYPNOSIS

Hypnosis is also an effective treatment for bed-wetting. However, it must be performed by a properly trained physician or psychologist.

THE CHILD'S RESPONSIBILITY

Children over the age of seven who wet the bed are old enough to be responsible for washing their own pajamas and bedclothes. This should be done in a matter-of-fact way, without belittling, teasing, or putting the child down in any way. If the child's bed is wet and the child has forgotten to wash the pajamas and bedclothes, calmly remind him/her of what must be done.

PREVENTING BED-WETTING

To try to prevent bed-wetting, have the child go to the toilet before going to bed, limit late-night liquids, and do not awaken the child during the night. The goal is to eliminate the problem for good, not merely to have one night with a dry bed. If the child's bed happens to be dry, parents should praise him/her without mentioning the problem. Say something like, "You must be proud of yourself!" Finally, remain calm.

REMEMBER...

✔ Be calm.
✔ Make sure your child has a medical evaluation.
✔ After the age of seven, bed-wetting may be associated with emotional problems.

From: _____

COMING HOME ON TIME
Help children police themselves.

Dinner was at 5:30. Where were you?
You said you'd be home by 5:00 so you could do your homework before your game.

Children coming home on time is an issue most households have to face. Children say they'll be home, parents wait, and the children don't appear. Missed appointments, cold dinners, unfinished chores, and other aggravations make this an important problem to solve.

PAY BACK

When a child under the age of 14 comes home late, point out the lateness, but don't criticize him/her. Do not say or do anything else at that time. However, the next time the youngster wants to go out, he/she should be delayed for the same amount of time as he/she was late on the previous occasion. This payback system works because it makes sense to children. It is not viewed as a punishment as long as the parent is not critical.

This same approach can be used with older children. One of the problems with older children is that parents generally don't want to stay up to see when the child arrives home. A technique that solves this problem is to turn on the outside lights or perhaps a hall light and make it the teenager's responsibility to turn the light off when he/she arrives. Another effective method is to set an alarm clock in the hall and tell the child to turn it off upon arriving home. If the child doesn't get home on time and the alarm goes off, the parent is alerted that the child is not home. Set the alarm for five minutes after curfew. This allows for any discrepancy in the determination of the exact time. The next time the child wants to go out, the amount of late time must be paid back before he/she may leave the house.

Some parents attempt to punish children by making them come home early the next time they go out. This is often ineffective. Parents have no real control over when the child arrives. They do have control over the time the child leaves. Parents should always attempt to exercise control where they have the greatest advantage.

GROUNDING

An appropriate practice is to restrict the child from using the telephone or leaving the house for one day for each 15 minutes he/she was late. This should be explained to the child when the curfew is set. Then, if the child deliberately chooses to violate the curfew, the price paid is no surprise. If circumstances beyond the child's control put him/her in danger of being late, he/she should be expected to call home.

MISSED MEALS

If dinner is scheduled for a certain time and the child is not present, the family should eat without him/her. If the child arrives after dinner has been finished, his/her next meal should be breakfast, with no bedtime snack. If the child arrives during the meal, then the child can wait until everyone else has finished and eat alone without television or family conversation.

REMEMBER...

✔ Don't criticize, instead take action.
✔ Use the payback principle.
✔ Grounding can be effective.

From:

DAWDLING

Giving attention to dawdling actually makes it worse.

Most problems with dawdling are created, without awareness, by parents who are attempting to teach children to be prompt. This is the way it often happens: A child doesn't act promptly, so the parent starts to fuss. This gives the child attention, and the child quickly learns that by procrastinating he/she will receive a lot of attention. The attention is negative attention, but, to the child, that doesn't make any difference. Consequently, parents must be careful not to create a problem where one might not otherwise occur.

Dawdling must be addressed very early in the child's development. If not, it tends to become a habit and a way of life. In order to prevent this, parents need to take steps as soon as the problem is recognized. It is too easy for parents to step in and do whatever they're waiting for the child to do. In the parent's mind, this is more efficient and saves time. However, in the long run, it is wiser to take the necessary time to prevent or solve the problem.

The rule of thumb is: Don't do for children what they are capable of doing for themselves. Doing things for children that they can do for themselves merely fosters incompetence.

DON'T SAY "HURRY UP!"

When a child dawdles, the tendency is to say, "Hurry up!" This works if it is only said once. Unfortunately, in most cases, it is repeated over and over. Parents think urging motivates their children, but this type of interaction actually encourages dawdling.

PLAY A GAME

If a child is slow at getting things done, an effective way to hurry him/her up is to play a game. One game is to tell the child that if he/she can finish whatever needs to be done within five minutes the child will earn a reward. The reward should be something simple, like a lollipop or raisins. Another game is to bet the child that you can do whatever you need to do before the child can do his/her task. A third game is to bet the child that the task cannot be accomplished by a certain time. While the child is hurrying to complete the task, the parent should give the child both feedback and encouragement. Say, "You are really getting this job done fast!" or "You must be pleased with the good job you are doing!"

CATCH YOUR CHILD BEING PROMPT

If children are recognized for their promptness, they learn to be prompt. On the other hand, if children are given any attention, even negative, for dawdling, this is the behavior they tend to develop. Consequently, the importance of catching children when they are prompt and recognizing them for their promptness cannot be overemphasized. For example, if Johnny arrives on time, tell him how much you appreciate his ability to be on time and how proud he must be of himself.

REMEMBER...

✔ Don't say, "Hurry Up!"
✔ Make the task a game.
✔ Recognize and praise promptness.

© 1998 MAR+CO PRODUCTS, INC.

From:

DEMANDS
Do not grease the squeaky wheel.

Children are very clever at finding ways to demand attention. They may ask several questions or continually ask for one thing or another. They might act in more subtle ways by forgetting their lunch money, schoolbooks, homework, etc. There are any number of ways in which children make demands on a parent's time and attention.

"NO" MEANS "NO"

Human nature is such that the squeaky wheel usually gets the grease. Children are squeaky wheels when they badger parents until they give in just so they can have peace and quiet. Unfortunately, this only reinforces negative behavior. Children must learn that *no* means just that. Parents should decide the first time they hear a request whether or not to grant it. If the decision is not to grant the child's request, then no amount of badgering or begging should cause the parent to change his/her mind. Giving in to demands teaches children to be demanding.

BAILING CHILDREN OUT

When children forget something and parents bail them out, children learn it is not important for them to remember things. The frantic telephone call that lunch money, a library book, or gym clothes are at home often brings a parent running to school. When children demand and get attention from parents in this fashion, it is time to apply natural consequences. Natural consequences state that if children are irresponsible, parents do not bail them out. In other words, forgetting to take lunch money, gym clothes, or library books to school results in the child accepting the consequences set up by the school for these failures. Not rescuing children is difficult for many parents, because they want their children to be successful. What they fail to see is that in order for children to be successful, they must also be responsible.

HAVING A SHADOW

Some very young children make demands without saying a word. They are just always underfoot. A parent might hardly be able to move without bumping into the child. Some children will even go so far as to hold onto a parent's leg. Parents need to learn to ignore children who behave is such inappropriate ways, and eventually, the shadowing or clinging will cease. If you are not willing to tolerate the shadowing or clinging, then remove the child to a safe and appropriate place for a specific amount of time.

RECOGNIZING A DEMANDING CHILD

When parents feel pressured by a child, it is a good indication that the child is being demanding. Parents must trust their feelings, recognize the cause of the situation, and take immediate steps to ignore it. If the demands begin to work on your nerves, then it is time to get away from the child. Escaping to another room, putting on a set of headphones, or getting your spouse to take over while you go for a walk are ways to avoid a demanding child and still save your sanity.

REMEMBER...

✔ Do not give in to demands—ignore them.
✔ The more you talk to the child the less likely it is that the demands will stop.
✔ If demands begin to work on your nerves, get away from the child for a time.

From:

FEAR OF DARKNESS

Don't attempt to force children to deal with the dark without making the darkness less scary for them.

It is common for children to develop fears of the dark. Parents may believe that forcing children to experience darkness will help them get used to it. This is a mistake. Another mistake is to give in to the child's wishes by letting him/her sleep with the light on, sleep in the parents' bed, or to sit beside the bed until the child is asleep. While this may be acceptable to the parents, it merely reinforces the child's belief that there is a real reason to be afraid of the dark.

TALK ABOUT THE FEAR

Parents should explain that they understand this fear and encourage their children to talk about it. During the conversation, parents should tell their children that they, or someone they knew, were afraid of the dark, too, when they were young. However, now that they are grown, they realize there is nothing to fear. Parents should inform their children that they will be close by, perhaps even in the next room. Above all, parents should not stay in the bedroom with the child. This merely reinforces the fear. They should explain there is a rule in the house when people go to bed the lights are turned out.

FUN IN THE DARK

To prevent the fear of darkness from arising, parents can, very early in their children's development, expose them to darkness as a time when they can have fun. Parents and children may play games together in a dark room. *Hide and Seek* in the dark or pretending to be cave people who had no lights are good examples of such games. Parents and children may also go outside in the dark and sit there together for a time. If children experience darkness when they are having fun and feel secure, the fear of darkness is not likely to occur.

OTHER TECHNIQUES

Invite one of the child's friends to spend the night, thereby encouraging the child to sleep in a dark room. Of course, be careful not to select a friend who is afraid of the dark.

Put some fluorescent stickers or stars on the ceiling of the child's room.

Put a flashlight by the child's bed and teach him/her how to turn it on.

Gradually decrease the amount of light in the child's room. This may be done by using a dimmer switch or by moving a small light farther and farther away from the child's bed.

REMEMBER...

✔ Take preventative steps—play in the dark.
✔ Tell the child, "When I got big, I realized there was no reason to fear the dark."
✔ Gradually decrease the amount of light in the child's room.

From:

FIGHTING (PHYSICAL AND VERBAL)

Sometimes encouraging inappropriate behavior actually eliminates it.

Most fights occur in the hope that Mom or Dad will intervene and side with the child instigating the fight. Regardless of the purpose behind the fight, verbal and physical fighting between siblings is nerve-wracking to parents. Parents want their children to get along, and fighting can upset the entire household. If you have tried different methods to get your children to stop fighting and none of them have worked, you might want to consider *encouraging* the behavior. This may sound ridiculous, but it may be just what is needed to change your home from a battleground into a peaceful place to live.

GO OUTSIDE

One way to handle fighting is to tell children, "If you want to fight, you have to go outside." Once outside, the fighting seldom continues. Why? The purpose of most fights is to gain a parent's attention or support and the purpose is gone when the parent is no longer in sight. If one child is weaker than another, that child will probably not put him/herself into this situation without hope of rescue.

RESTRICTED FIGHTING TIMES

If desired, parents can set aside a 15-minute period each day when their children are permitted to fight. Tell the children that this is the only time of the day when they are allowed to fight. If they begin to fight before the designated time, remind them of the rule. When the time for the fight arrives, bring the children together. Tell them this is the time to fight. This technique is nearly always effective in eliminating any desire the children may have had to fight. It seems that when fights are structured, they lose their appeal. Many children feel that when they get into a fight, their parents will rescue them. This approach bypasses that possibility.

YOUNGER VERSUS OLDER CHILD

Many sibling fights result from a younger child picking on an older child. In most cases, the parent will punish the older child, saying, "You should know better." When this occurs, younger children learn they can pick fights without any consequences. They know how to get an older sibling into trouble and know they do not have to be responsible for their behavior. Older children then decide that Mom and Dad are not always fair and devise ways to get even with the younger sibling. These are not behaviors parents want their children to learn. Parents want harmony and cooperation.

When using the *Go Outside*, *Restricted Fighting Times*, or *Younger Versus Older Child* methods, the parent should place him/herself in an inconspicuous viewing position and step in if necessary.

TREAT CHILDREN AS EQUALS

To achieve harmony, follow the rule that everyone involved in the fight gets the same punishment. Unless a parent is 100% certain that the fight is totally the fault of one child, treat all children the same way. Another potential good may come out of imposing the same punishment on all: All the children now share the same problem. This tends to bring them together.

REMEMBER...

- ✔ Do not side with one child.
- ✔ Everyone involved in the fight receives the same punishment.
- ✔ Don't give fighting children an audience.

© 1998 MAR+CO PRODUCTS, INC.

From:

HYPERACTIVITY

If you can, keep your head when all about you are losing theirs... Kipling

Hyperactive children and their parents are often in conflict. It is important to remember not to scold, but to take effective action.

HYPERACTIVE OR HYPERKINETIC?

The first distinction to be made is whether a child is *hyperactive* or *hyperkinetic*. The child who is hyperactive has what appears to be a chemical deficiency in the brain which won't allow him/her to function normally. The hyperkinetic child, on the other hand, has the appropriate level of chemicals. This child is overly active because he/she has either never learned appropriate behavior, has actually been encouraged to be overly active, or is highly anxious.

Professionals use special techniques to distinguish between children who are hyperactive and children who are hyperkinetic. As a parent, you may be able to make the distinction by asking yourself if there are any conditions or times when your child can remain still for 15 minutes. The hyperactive child has total inability to sit still. The hyperkinetic child can, at times, be quiet and sit still. This 15-minute suggestion is only a guideline.

LENGTHENING ATTENTION SPAN

One of the main goals for a child who is either hyperactive or hyperkinetic is developing a longer attention span. Parents must start at the child's level, and gradually work to have the child pay attention for longer and longer periods of time. This can frequently be done by giving the child attention as long as he/she attends to the task at hand. Playing a game by saying, "I'll bet you can't keep coloring until lunchtime," or "I bet you can't keep your eyes on the book and read until the alarm goes off." These are the type of statements that motivate a child to make an extra effort.

ACTIVITY LEVEL

A second area that needs to be addressed is the child's activity level. It is important that parents model a calm activity level. This can be difficult, as these children can cause parents to become hyper themselves. If you feel this happening to you, remove yourself from the situation until you calm down and feel under control.

SOCIAL SKILLS

Another area in which these children need training is in getting along with people. Provide the child with opportunities in which he/she can get along with others. Make suggestions about how to win friends.

Invite only one child at a time to play for a specified time period. Supervise the children from a distance. Provide a snack during the close of playtime. Discuss the playtime with the child, praising his/her positive interactions with the other child. If any problems occurred, have the child suggest other ways he/she could have handled the situation.

REMEMBER...

✔ Do not model hyperactivity.
✔ Teach the child appropriate behavior; don't just criticize.
✔ A truly hyperactive child may need an evaluation by a pediatrician or child psychologist.

From:

INTERRUPTIONS

Ignore interruptions and they will almost always cease.

You are talking on the telephone. Before the conversation has ended, your child has asked you one or more questions.

You are talking to a friend in a store and your child is pulling on your clothes.

Many children attempt to get attention by constantly interrupting parents, other adults, or other children. Sometimes they do this by asking questions or making some type of physical gesture, such as pulling on one's clothing or hand. When children interrupt, they are almost always attempting to get attention. This usually gets reinforced when the parent tells the child to stop or responds to the interruption by answering the question. When parents do this, it teaches children interrupting is acceptable.

To stop interruptions, parents must ignore the behavior. If clothes are being pulled, ignore the action and walk away. If questions are being asked, develop a "deaf ear." Treat interruptions as if they didn't exist. When handled this way, the behavior usually doesn't last very long. When the child does not get the desired attention, the behavior does not get reinforced.

THE CONTINUING INTERRUPTION

Sometimes interruptions persist for so long that the parent's nerves are becoming frazzled. This is the time to revert to *time out*. Send the child to a room or chair for a period of time. If the parent isn't able to use a *time-out* procedure for the child, then it is time for the parent to escape. Walking away from the child or turning up the radio or television will enable the parent to ignore the child's interruptions.

BEHAVIOR CHANGES TAKE TIME

Don't expect ignoring the child's behavior to produce immediate results. It will probably take two or three weeks before improvement is apparent. It will also take being consistent and *not* giving in to your child. Every time you give in, you reinforce the interrupting behavior. Parents must be strong.

GIVE ATTENTION FOR APPROPRIATE BEHAVIORS

Children need attention, but they have to learn how to get it in an appropriate fashion. Most children's bad or inappropriate behaviors occur as a result of their attempts to get attention and recognition. When a behavior, whether good or bad, is recognized, it is likely to be repeated and used the next time children want attention. Therefore, it is important to reinforce only *desirable* behaviors. Select a time when the child has been good to initiate some special interaction, such as: reading a story, playing a game, or making something with the child.

No matter how often you engage in these positive attention activities, there will probably be times when your child will attempt to get your attention by using inappropriate interruptions. Just don't give in at those times.

REMEMBER...

✔ Interruptions are designed to get attention.
✔ Don't let yourself become frazzled.
✔ Ignore, ignore, ignore.

From:

LEAVING TOYS OUT OF PLACE

Children should be taught proper behavior and then expected to perform at the level of their ability.

Children need to learn a sense of responsibility and neatness and one of the very first teaching opportunities involves picking up toys. Insist that children pick up their toys. Resist the temptation to do it for the child because you can do it faster.

TEACH WHAT YOU EXPECT TO BE DONE

If you want your children to pick up their toys, there are several things you must do. First, you must show your child what must be done. Once the child has begun picking up his/her toys, it is important to praise your child by making statements such as, "You're doing a good job, Scott," or "That's the way, Maria, that's exactly the way to do it." Hearing positive comments from a parent encourages a child to continue the behavior.

When your child has his/her toys picked up, it is a good idea to permit him/her to overhear you telling another family member what happened and how you felt. You might say, "You should have seen the good job that Ray did picking up his toys this afternoon. I was very proud of him."

WHEN TOYS ARE NOT PICKED UP

There will be times when children, even after they have been taught what to do, refuse or forget to pick up their toys. If it becomes necessary to ask your child to pick up the toys, do not ask more than once. If you find yourself on the verge of asking a second time, it is time to use time-out or restrict some type of privilege until the toys have been put away properly.

A related technique is the Jail Box. Whenever anyone in the family finds something out of place, that item is "arrested" and put in jail. All items remain in the box for one week. If someone in the family needs to use something that is jailed, the item can be purchased by children for 25¢ and by adults for $5.00. The money is put into a fund that will finance an outing for the whole family.

REMEMBER THE POWER OF PRAISE

One of the biggest mistakes parents make is failing to praise children for picking up their toys. On the other hand, children who don't pick up their toys get all kinds of attention. Remember that even negative attention, from a child's point of view, is better than no attention at all. When you give children attention, even if it is criticism for not picking up their toys, you actually discourage them from picking up their toys in the future.

REMEMBER...

✔ Teach children early in life how to pick up their toys.
✔ Don't pick up your child's toys just to save time.
✔ Compliment children when they pick up their toys.

From: _____

LYING

Attempting to force a child to tell the truth encourages further lying.

Parents want their children to be truthful. So, when children lie, most parents feel compelled to force them to tell the truth. It is as if telling the truth has some magical power for preventing future lies. Also, for some reason, many parents seem to think that if the child owns up to something, the situation will never be repeated. Unfortunately, this is not necessarily true. In fact, experience tends to indicate that the more parents pressure children to tell the truth, the more they encourage further lying.

WHY CHILDREN LIE

Some children lie to avoid punishment. Others lie in order to get attention and recognition.

LYING TO AVOID PUNISHMENT

A parent's behavior can teach children that lying is better than telling the truth. If a child breaks a lamp, admits the truth, and receives a punishment, the child learns it would have been better to lie. The wise parent says, "I'm sure you didn't mean to break the lamp, and I know you are going to be more careful in the future." or "I'm going to have to buy a new lamp, and I want you to pay for part of the cost." If the child has no money, work out a way for the child to earn some money by working around the house. Children who are recognized for telling the truth grow up to be truthful.

LYING TO GET ATTENTION

Some lies are told in order to get attention. Many times, children learn that the more fantastic the lie, the more attention they seem to get.

MAKE A DECISION

Question the child about the situation once, and only once. If the child appears to be lying, a parent must make a decision to accept what the child says, even though there are some doubts, or to treat what he/she said as a lie. The important point here is that the parent must make the decision, rather than attempting to pressure the child into telling the truth. If there is a fair probability that the child is telling the truth, the parent should treat the child's statement as the truth and drop the issue without bringing it up again.

NEVER CALL A CHILD A LIAR

If, after hearing the child's explanation, the parent decides there is a very high probability the child is lying, then the parent should decide how to treat the situation. Above all, do not call the child a liar. One way to encourage lying is to accuse someone of it. The accused has a tendency to say, "Well, they think that I am lying anyhow, so I may as well go ahead and do it." One appropriate way of treating lying is to take away some privilege or activity that the child enjoys for the remainder of the day.

REMEMBER...

✔ Do not pressure a child to own up to a wrong.
✔ Talk about the situation only once, then decide to drop it or to impose some restriction.
✔ Never call the child a liar.

© 1998 MAR+CO PRODUCTS, INC.

From:

NAIL-BITING
A habit that needs to be treated as a habit.

In most cases, fingernail-biting occurs because children are nervous or anxious. Sometimes they begin nail-biting in order to imitate someone else. In rare cases, nail-biting may signal a deep emotional problem which requires counseling.

BREAKING THE HABIT

Three ways to help children break the nail-biting habit are:

1. Purchase an over-the-counter product that deters nail-biting and apply it to the child's fingernails to serve as a reminder. Ask your pharmacist what would be good to use with children.
2. Don't criticize or tell children not to bite their fingernails. This makes them more nervous and causes them to bite their nails even more.
3. Recognize any improvement that occurs. For example, say, "Johnny, it looks like that finger is beginning to get a nice nail on it."

CHANGING A HABIT

To change any habit, it is necessary to change as many of the behaviors and circumstances associated with it as possible. For example, there are almost surely certain things that the child does while chewing fingernails—perhaps lying in bed with a blanket, doing homework, or watching TV. There are also certain behaviors that have occurred just before the child began biting his/her nails, perhaps getting ready for bed or after finishing a meal. Parents should first identify these times, and then change them.

It is not always possible to change all the preceding behaviors or circumstances, but in nearly every case, *something* can be changed. It is important for parents to do what they can to change things. Even changing to a different blanket, having a story time, changing the child's bedtime, or changing the room in which homework is done can help eliminate the habit. Changing the situation by scheduling something to occur either earlier or later is wise. If the problem occurs frequently after a meal, have the child help clear the table. Remember: The key is to interrupt the nail-biting without saying anything about the nail-biting itself.

CHECK WITH YOUR CHILD

Ask your child if he/she wants to change the habit. If the answer is *no*, then leave it alone for the time being. Bring the subject up again at a later date, when he/she might be more receptive to the idea.

Generally, parents cannot force a child to change a habit. Even if they do, the price paid is more than victory is worth. Bide your time, as almost every child will eventually decide to eliminate the habit.

REMEMBER...

✔ Do not criticize or call attention to the nail-biting.
✔ Identify the circumstances and behaviors preceding the nail-biting and change the ones you can.
✔ Don't try to change this behavior unless the child wants to change it.

From:

NAME-CALLING/BEING PICKED ON
Teach your child not to show anger or hurt.

Children pick on other children. They find opportunities to be cruel in spite of a parent's or teacher's best efforts to prevent it.

Unfortunately, the child being picked on has a difficult time and the situation often begins to affect his/her self-concept, emotions, and school performance. For the child's emotional and academic well-being, it is necessary for parents to know how to deal with this problem.

SABOTAGE THE PAYOFF

Children need to know and understand that the payoff for any name-caller is for the child being teased to become upset. Tell your child, "Whenever you get upset, that is exactly what the person doing the name-calling wants. Are you going to let that person upset you?" To prevent the payoff, your child must learn not to become visibly upset. He/She must be convinced that ignoring the bully will eventually cause the behavior to stop.

Most children find it hard to ignore name-calling. They are hurt and angry. If it cannot be ignored, they can make a joke of the name-calling or change the subject. When children being picked on do or say something funny, they frequently change the other children's attitudes toward them and the name-calling usually ceases to be a problem. A child who was teased and called a snake made a hissing sound, laughed, and walked away. In other words, try to find out what name the child is being called and, if appropriate, teach him/her a way to actually exaggerate the name-calling. This shows everyone that the person being teased is not bothered by the name.

Changing the subject can also work. When the name is called, have the child answer by asking a question that is in no way connected to the name being called. A child may ask a question about an upcoming holiday, a school game, or even about an assignment. This will usually confuse the name-caller and the question may be answered or the child may choose to ask the question, not wait for an answer, and walk away. Do not let the name-caller see any hurt and anger.

WHEN DOES NAME-CALLING END?

The key to this issue is convincing the child being teased that he/she is the only one who can really change the situation. If they feel it is a parent's, teacher's, or someone else's responsibility, there is not much hope.

If the child can ignore, make a joke of name-calling, or change the subject it doesn't usually continue for very long. Children must not expect that ignoring the name-calling will solve the problem immediately. However, they can usually eliminate the name-calling within a couple of weeks.

REMEMBER...

✔ Ignore name-calling. Show no evidence of hurt.
✔ Make a joke of name-calling.
✔ Do not get angry. Smile instead.

From:

NIGHTMARES

Fantasy causes them. Magic will eliminate them.

The resistance children show when going to sleep is often their fear of having nightmares. Children sometimes awaken during the night crying and upset because of a bad dream. Parents sometimes cope with this situation by allowing the child to sleep in their bed. This is a mistake.

MAGIC TV TECHNIQUE

An effective way to solve the nightmare problem is by using the Magic TV Technique. As you tuck your child into bed, ask, "Have I ever told you about the Magic TV? It is wonderful! Inside our heads each of us has a Magic TV. The Magic TV is your *mind*, and it allows you to think about lots of different things. You can think about our dog. You can think about our last vacation, or about anything you want. The TV in our family room has only a few channels, but your Magic TV has thousands of channels. On the TV in our family room, we can only watch the programs that are being shown at that time. The TV in our heads is different. It's magic because we can turn on any program we want, any time we want, to watch it. Isn't that great? I have a Magic TV in my head and you do, too. Try using yours." Say, "Turn on (PICK SOMETHING THE CHILD CAN VISUALIZE AND RELATE TO)." After about five seconds, say, "Now, turn on (SELECT SOMETHING ELSE)." Check to be sure your child was able to visualize the topics. Then continue telling the child to turn the channels and "see" enjoyable memories. Next, have your child suggest things. Once the Magic TV Technique is understood, say, "Why don't you think about all the fun things you have done? Before long, it will be morning." At this point, leave the room.

In most cases, the Magic TV Technique works the very first night. However, even if the nightmare occurs again, reassure your child that the Magic TV will work.

DON'T EMPHASIZE THE NIGHTMARE

Do not focus on the nightmare. Do not ask the child if he/she has had one. If your child tells you about a nightmare, don't discuss it. Simply say that the Magic TV will make the nightmares go away. If you can tell your child about a time the Magic TV did work, it will make the technique more effective.

OLDER CHILDREN, TEENAGERS, AND ADULTS

This technique also works for older children, teenagers, and adults. Although older children and adults may not have nightmares, they do have worries that sometimes interfere with sleep. Knowing how to turn on the "good channels" is fun and can reduce stress.

REMEMBER...
✔ Do not ask about or discuss nightmares.
✔ Teach your child about the Magic TV.
✔ Help the child focus on pleasant things.

PAIN

Focus your child's attention on something other than the pain.

Most of the pain we experience is due to stress and tension. Only a small portion of it is actually due to physical tissue damage. Consequently, the manner in which your mind focuses on the damaged area has a tremendous influence on how much physical pain you feel. For example, a child falls and skins his knee, runs all the way home without a whimper, and, as soon as he gets home, begins to scream as if he were dying. This happens because the child is initially so focused on getting to safety that he isn't thinking about the pain. When the child reaches home, he is no longer worried about getting to safety. The child's attention turns to the painful area.

DISTRACTION TECHNIQUES

One way to decrease a child's perception of pain is by distracting him/her. For example, while washing a child's cut, you might say, *"Look, how beautiful it is outside today. Do you see that large tree? Can you guess what kind of tree it is?"* This kind of approach will enable the child to think less about the pain by focusing on something pleasant.

There are other ways to redirect a child's attention. One way is to simply ask the child to close his/her eyes and picture being involved in the fun activity you are going to describe.

The relaxation approach also works with some children. To use this technique, the child must listen carefully to what you are saying and believe what he/she is hearing is actually happening. Tell the child to imagine he/she is beginning to get sleepy, his/her arms are getting heavy, etc. After mentioning several body parts, tell the child his/her whole body is getting tired and sleepy. He/she will begin to feel numb and become calmer and calmer. Repeating these phrases allows the child to relax, and relaxation will reduce the pain.

Another distraction technique is to give the child something he/she wants such as an ice-cream cone. Any technique that helps distract the child's attention from the painful area and focus it on something else will help to alleviate the child's pain.

REASSURANCE

It is important to direct the child's attention away from the pain, but it is also important to make the child feel he/she is healthy and will be fine. An adult who gets hurt becomes worried and fearful about his/her physical well-being. This increases stress and tension. Children react the same way, and that is why it is so important to reassure them they will be fine. Once they have been reassured, they feel less stress and tension. This, in turn, reduces the pain and facilitates the child's physical recovery. A word of caution: Do not overdo it. Too much reassurance may make the child doubt what you are saying. Simply tell the child once or twice, in a calm voice, that he/she will be fine.

REMEMBER...

✔ Fear increases pain.
✔ Calm reassurance decreases pain.
✔ Relaxation and distraction reduce pain.

© 1998 MAR+CO PRODUCTS, INC.

From:

POOR EATING HABITS

You can lead a horse to water, but you can't make it drink.

Parents are concerned about their children's nutrition. That is the reason they encourage children to eat the right foods. However, children do not always cooperate. They sometimes refuse to eat foods that are nutritious, and the result is a battle between children and parents. A parent may force the child to eat, but this is merely going to create an antagonistic situation and probably turn the child more and more against that particular food. Besides, a parent can't force a child to eat all of the time.

METHODS TO AVOID

Parents should avoid making the mistake of trying to explain the importance of eating a particular food. Also, the more parents give the impression of trying to urge, pressure, or persuade the child to eat, the more resistant the child is probably going to become.

METHODS TO USE

Parents may try one of the following approaches:

1. Tell the child he/she isn't old enough to eat a particular food. For example, "I'm sorry, Johnny. I should have known better than to serve you this food. You aren't old enough to eat it yet." This frequently will result in the child proving he/she *is* old enough.
2. Pair the food you want the child to start eating with one of his/her favorite foods. For example, if a child doesn't like potatoes but does like cheese, fix potatoes and then melt some cheese in with them. At first, the predominant taste must be cheese. Over time, gradually start using less cheese, so the child will eventually be eating only potatoes. Using this procedure, a parent can teach a child to like almost any food. The mistakes made in this approach, however, are skimping on the desirable food or trying to change the child too quickly. Patience will pay off if you use this method.

REVENGE AND ASSERTING INDEPENDENCE

Two of the main reasons children don't eat certain foods are because they have a sense that refusing to eat them is a way of getting back at their parents or they are showing their own independence. If left on their own, many children might eat a particular food, but since a parent has made an issue of it, they stubbornly refuse.

NOT EATING AT ALL

Don't pressure a child who refuses to eat anything. Eventually, hunger will solve the problem. After a day or two, hunger will usually persuade the child to start eating proper foods. Don't worry unless the child's lack of eating has resulted in a 10% loss of weight. If that happens, seek professional help. Don't allow the child to eat only "junk foods," rationalizing, "Well, at least he is eating *something*."

REMEMBER...

- ✔ Avoid making mealtime a battleground.
- ✔ Curtail "junk-food" eating.
- ✔ Pair the food you want the child to eat with one of his/her favorites.

From: _____

SCREAMING

Attempts to stop or prevent screaming usually make it worse.

Children generally scream in an attempt to get attention or to get their own way. The screaming becomes a control mechanism to either embarrass the parent in a public place or to get the parent's attention if no one else is around. If a parent gives in to a child's screams, the child will feel encouraged to repeat the behavior. The best thing a parent can do when a child begins to scream (provided the child is not hurt, injured, or sick) is to totally and completely ignore the behavior.

SCREAMING IS NERVE-WRACKING

Ignoring a screaming child can be nerve-wracking and requires a great deal of self-discipline on the part of a parent. Children often choose to scream in public because they can get a great deal of mileage out of the behavior and usually get their own way. Parents become embarrassed and will do almost anything to get the screaming to stop. Even at home, screaming can get on a parent's nerves so badly that he/she will give in just to gain some peace and quiet. Every time a parent gives in to screaming, a child learns that screaming pays off. Once that lesson is learned, parents can be assured that the behavior will be repeated again and again.

UNCONTROLLABLE SCREAMING

Some children get themselves so worked up that they can't hear what you say. When this happens, anything you do to try to gain the child's cooperation only makes the situation worse. A parent trying to stop a child from screaming is like a person trying to put out a fire by throwing gasoline on it.

In these situations, parents need step to back and ignore the screaming child. They should give the child the impression they are gone, but keep the child in sight from behind the door, or some other appropriate place to insure the child is safe. After the child has calmed down, the parent should wait another two or three minutes, and then approach the child as if the screaming had never happened. As quickly as possible, get the child involved in some activity.

DON'T BE MISLED

Screaming sometimes stops when a parent corrects a screaming child. If the child does not scream again, the parent's strategy has been successful. However, if the screaming starts again later, the parents' action was not effective. It is important for the behavior to stop on more than a temporary basis. The best way to achieve this result is by developing a "deaf ear."

REMEMBER...

✔ Ignore the child's behavior.
✔ Remain calm.
✔ Be careful not to be misled by short-term results.

© 1998 MAR*CO PRODUCTS, INC.

From:

STEALING

Forget trying to get a child to admit he/she has taken something.

Attempting to get children to admit they have taken something that belongs to someone else is usually futile. Children know stealing is wrong. It is hard for a child who has stolen something to admit he/she has done something wrong. Ask the child about it only once. If the child denies having stolen anything, don't press the issue.

WAS SOMETHING STOLEN?

Parents must decide in their own minds whether their child is likely to have taken the item. If there is a 95% probability that the child stole something, parents should decide what type of approach to use and what, if any, punishment to give the child.

If there is any major uncertainty about whether the child took the item, parents should give him/her the benefit of the doubt and drop the issue. Most parents make the mistake of trying to pressure the child in hopes that he/she will finally break down and tell the truth.

DEALING WITH STEALING

If a parent assumes that his/her child did steal something, some appropriate reactions are:

- Telling the child, "Although you have denied taking the object, I have good reason to suspect that you did take it. Because of this, you are restricted to your room for two nights."
- Taking away privileges such as TV or going out to play.
- Telling the child he/she may not go to a major event he/she was planning to attend.

If, at this point, the child insists he/she is innocent, tell the child one more time that you have to act on what the situation appears to be. Explain that if it turns out you are wrong, you will apologize. Do not discuss the matter with the child again, but move to implement any punishment or restriction.

If the child admits to having taken something that belongs to someone other than yourself, he/she should be instructed to return the item to its rightful owner. This step applies even if the child stole the item from a department store or from a neighbor. Forcing the child to face the neighbor or department-store owner is perhaps the best corrective measure a parent can use in a situation like this. There is usually no need for additional punishment.

If the child steals a second time, repeat the procedure. This time, however, additional restriction may be in order. In the vast majority of cases, this procedure will solve the problem. However, if the stealing doesn't stop, the child should be taken to a counselor or psychologist.

REMEMBER...

✔ Do not press the child for an admission of guilt.
✔ Parents decide the fate (either to forget or to punish).
✔ Have the child return the stolen item and face the owner.

From:

STUTTERING

Stuttering is usually emotionally based.

Why children develop stuttering is not fully understood, but it is known that stuttering usually relates to feelings of pressure or stress. Many efforts to help stutterers actually increase the stress and make the stuttering worse. If you have a child who stutters:

1. Don't appear to be overly concerned. This is apt to make the stuttering worse.
2. Do everything you can to prevent other children from making fun of your child.
3. When your child begins to talk, give him/her your undivided attention and don't interrupt even to correct your child.

CONFIDENCE

The child must feel confident that he/she can speak plainly. Be careful not to undermine your child's confidence and reinforce the problem. Do not say anything about the stuttering unless your child expresses concern about it. When responding to your child's concern, use positive statements, such as, "I've noticed—it is getting better." This will help to build your child's confidence.

MODEL GOOD SPEECH

It is important for people in your child's environment to speak properly and clearly. A parent who has a stuttering problem is much more likely to have children who stutter.

STRESS AND PRESSURE

Many children grow out of stuttering on their own. Others need speech therapy. Some may even need psychological counseling. If the stuttering seems to be triggered by a feeling of pressure or stress, the child may need to learn how to deal with stress.

Stuttering may continue after the stressors disappear or the child has learned better ways to deal with stress. Sometimes stuttering has become such a habit that it continues out of the habit rather than a result of pressures or stress.

HELPFUL TECHNIQUES

If your child stutters when answering the phone, have him/her practice "answering" the phone when there is no incoming call. If practice is a method you wish to use, the practice situation should be closely related to the real situation.

Try to get your child to forget or at least not focus on what is probably going to happen next. There is a tendency for children to anticipate stuttering in future situations. Get your child's mind on something else. When this happens, children often stop stuttering.

Children who stutter when they speak often do not stutter when they sing. If this is true of your child, teach him/her to begin the first statement with a sing-song melody and then change to normal speech.

REMEMBER...

✔ Don't correct children who stutter or show negative concern.
✔ Try to identify if stress or fear is a factor in your child's stuttering.
✔ Undermining your child's confidence will reinforce the problem.

© 1998 MAR+CO PRODUCTS, INC.

From: _____

TALKING BACK

Be careful not to win the battle at the expense of losing the war.

Children talk back in order to place themselves in positions of recognition and authority. Remember that a child who can get a parent to argue with him/her feels a sense of power. If the parent does not argue back, the child is in a powerless position. Not arguing tells the child that the comment that was made did not even warrant a response. This puts children in their place better than any words the parent could say.

IGNORE

Generally, it is best to ignore children when they talk back. This is very difficult, because most parents feel their authority is being challenged and react in some way to what the child has said. This merely encourages the child to talk back even more. Children have even more power over their parents when they are in a public place. A parent's embarrassment gives the child more power, because the parent is likely to give in to bring the situation to an end. Children learn quickly when their attempts to gain power receive recognition.

A good behavioral principle to follow is: If something can be ignored, ignore it. If ignoring the child's behavior could cause harm to the child or someone else, action must taken. Many times, however, parents feel something must be done, when, in fact, the best approach is to take no action at all. Parents feel that they must intervene in order to teach the child something when what they actually teach is the very thing they wanted to prevent in the first place. Remember, children will learn to argue if they practice arguing or if arguing gets them what they want.

THE HARD STAND

Parents frequently think taking a hard stand will prevent their child from arguing in the future. In fact, this is the approach most parents take first. If it works, then the parents should hardly ever have to worry about the child talking back again. If the child continues to talk back and argue, the parent must realize that this approach is not working.

TAKING ACTION

If a situation cannot be ignored, take some action which does not include talking or discussion. An angry child does not want to *talk*. An angry child wants to *win*. Generally speaking, most parents talk too much when disciplining instead of focusing on trying to change behaviors. Taking action, in this type of situation, means depriving the child of some privilege. For example, "If you say one more word about this, you will have chosen to be restricted to your room."

REMEMBER...

✔ If you try something and it works for a while and then the behavior returns, it is not working.
✔ Ignore talking back whenever you can.
✔ Tell the child what the consequences of further talking back will be, and follow through if necessary.

From: _____

TARDINESS

Reward promptness, not tardiness.

Many children develop the habit of being late because they inadvertently get rewarded for their behavior. For example, a child who has dawdled misses the bus, so the parent drives him/her to school. When this happens, there is a fair chance the child will be late and miss the bus in the future.

Children are frequently rewarded when they arrive late for a meeting or activity. Upon arriving, everybody gives them attention. This extra attention given to the late arrival is quickly recognized as being more desirable than the lack of attention received when arriving early or on time. If parents want to prevent their children from being late, they must not reward for tardiness. Instead, they must reward for promptness.

NATURAL CONSEQUENCES

The best way to deal with tardiness is to let natural consequences take effect. If, as a result of lateness due to his/her own fault, the child misses out on something, no attempt should be made to compensate for the child's tardiness. Doing so leads the child to believe lateness is acceptable. Allowing natural consequences to run their course without parental intervention teaches children being late is not beneficial or acceptable.

Sometimes there are no natural negative consequences in the tardy situation. This is the time for a parent, no matter how distressed and worried, to ignore the child's lateness and make no comment or reference to it. If another child was prompt, recognize that child before the one who was tardy.

HURRY UP! YOU'RE GOING TO BE LATE!

Telling your child, "Hurry up! You're going to be late!" teaches that child to dawdle. When these kinds of comments are made, the child is getting a great deal of attention and actually being encouraged to dawdle.

PROMPTNESS CHART

Encourage promptness by keeping a record or chart. Mark it with a star or check for each time your child arrives promptly. Encourage the child to set a goal and choose a reward for reaching it. Parents should have several reasonable rewards in mind for the child to choose from, rather than allowing the child to pick any random reward.

NOTICE PROMPTNESS

No matter how tardy a child may consistently be, sooner or later he/she will accidentally be on time. When this occurs, it is very important that the child be given a great deal of attention and recognition. This will encourage him/her to be prompt in the future.

REMEMBER...

✔ Do not give recognition for tardiness.
✔ Identify consequences and follow through with them.
✔ Recognize promptness.

From: _____

TATTLING

Ignore tattling, but teach children when it is appropriate to tell on one another.

You want your children to inform you about serious matters, but you don't want them to tattle about small, insignificant issues.

TRAIN YOUR CHILD TO REPORT

Children need to be taught when they should report to you. The general rule of thumb is: If someone is hurt or might get hurt, or if somebody's property is going to be damaged, report it. Issues involving how your child gets along with another child or how other children are getting along should *not* be reported. Tell your child, "Settle that among yourselves."

One way to help your child understand what he/she should report is to ask your child a question such as, "If Mary Jane calls you a name once in awhile, should you tell me about that?" The answer is obviously *no*. If your child does not know the correct response, then teach it. Other examples of questions to ask your child are, "If Billy is throwing stones at cars, should it be reported? If Tammy cheats in a game, should that be reported? If Johnny is throwing stones at Mark, should that be reported?" By asking questions that refer to different behaviors, you can teach your child under what conditions it would be appropriate for him/her to report to you. Knowing when to report and when not to stops the constant tattling that many children do.

DEALING WITH TATTLING

If your child continues to tattle after proper training, you need to develop a "deaf ear." Either refuse to respond to your child or say, "Take care of it yourself." If you do not listen to or respond to tattling, it will not continue for very long.

Do not scold your child for tattling. That will merely make matters worse. Rather, develop that "deaf ear" and simply ignore any comments of a tattling nature. When your child begins to talk about something else, start interacting immediately. You want to give your child attention for behaving properly. Be careful *not* to give it for inappropriate behavior. When tattling is ignored, it seldom persists for very long. It is when children get attention or when they are able to get another person in trouble, that tattling is rewarded. Be careful not to make tattling an issue. Simply dismiss it and go on with whatever you were doing.

REMEMBER...

✔ Teach children when to report to you or another adult.
✔ Do not scold a child for tattling. Ignore the behavior.
✔ Tattling usually goes away if it is ignored.

From:

TEMPER TANTRUMS
If you ignore tantrums, they will usually disappear.

Most tantrums occur because adults have inadvertently or accidentally encouraged them. In other words, children have been taught that tantrums help them get what they want. The best way to deal with temper tantrums is to ignore them. If you find tantrums difficult to ignore because they are getting on your nerves, the best thing to do is to get away from them. Go into another room or out into the yard, but inconspicuously watch the child making sure he/she does not do anything dangerous. When there is no one around to pay attention to the tantrum, it quickly subsides. This is true of almost every type of tantrum. If a tantrum results in a dangerous or destructive situation, then time-out is a good technique to use.

TEMPER TANTRUMS IN A PUBLIC PLACE

Children frequently have temper tantrums in department stores or grocery stores. The tantrum usually begins with the parent refusing to do something the child wants. When children begin a tantrum in these situations, many advantages work in their favor. Parents, embarrassed at what they believe people may think, frequently give in to the tantrum by allowing a child to have what is wanted. When parents react in this way, they should ask themselves, "What have I taught my child?" The answer is that throwing tantrums is a way for them to get what they want. What a parent needs to do in this type of situation is ignore the child's behavior.

If the tantrum becomes very disruptive, then end the shopping, leaving potential purchases in the store and carrying the child to the car. The car then becomes a time-out room. In the car, the parent should not talk or reassure the child, as this encourages more tantrums. Just wait for the child to stop throwing the tantrum, then return to finish shopping. If the tantrum lasts very long, it would probably be best to simply forget about shopping at this time and return home.

GIVING UP IS GIVING IN

When a parent starts ignoring temper tantrums, the tantrums often become longer and harder. This is because the child thinks, "This used to work, but since it doesn't work now, I'd better try harder." At this point, parents may decide that ignoring the tantrums isn't working. This is a mistake. If parents do not continue to ignore tantrums, the child will be taught that such behavior is effective.

Another common mistake is to promise something to a child in exchange for stopping the tantrum. From a psychological viewpoint, this promise of a reward reinforces the tantrum behavior. The promise of a reward may stop the tantrum at that time, but greatly increases the likelihood of future tantrums.

REMEMBER...

✔ Ignore the child, if there is no danger.
✔ If the situation is dangerous, consider time-out.
✔ Never give in to a child throwing a tantrum.

From:

UNDESIRABLE FRIENDS

Attempts parents make to break up peer relationships may actually strengthen them.

One of the better ways of getting children to detach from certain peers is, on occasion, to simply raise questions such as: "Do you think Claire acts responsibly?" or "Do you think Mike is considerate of others?" Questions like these, if not asked too often, give children the opportunity to realize that some of their friends may have undesirable qualities.

AVOID NEGATIVE COMMENTS

Most of the mistakes parents make in dealing with their children's peers are in the form of making negative comments about them. Parents warn their children to stay away from certain friends and not have anything to do with them. This advice usually falls on "deaf ears" and makes the child more attached to the undesirable peers. Isn't it amazing how forbidden fruit has the most appeal? When parents make negative comments about a child's friends, the child usually feels compelled to become defensive. This strengthens the bond between the children. Consequently, a parent's attempt to break off a relationship usually reinforces it.

PEER INFLUENCE

Parents must realize that once a child reaches the age of 10, peers can become even more influential than parents in a child's life. When a child considers a peer an ideal or model, a parent must be very careful not to be overly critical of the person the child admires. Remember, children are not unlike adults. They, too, want to fit in and be accepted. Consequently, peer relationships become extremely important to them. As children become teenagers, most of them will gravitate toward their peers, even if it means being rejected by their parents.

INCLUSION IN FAMILY ACTIVITIES

If a child has a friend who isn't very acceptable to the family, it is wise to include that friend in family activities. Doing so deprives the child of an opportunity to rebel against the family's objection. It may also enable the family to find out that the child they think is so objectionable is not so bad after all. If the friend really is obnoxious, the child will begin to see that this friend doesn't fit in very well with the people who matter most to the child. The child usually arrives at this conclusion even if the parent's don't say anything about his/her friend's behavior.

REMEMBER...

✔ Don't put your child in a position where he/she has to defend a friend.
✔ Use subtle means to plant doubts in the child's mind about an undesirable friend.
✔ Invite the undesirable friend to join in a family activity. Be friendly to him/her.

PRE-ADOLESCENT AND ADOLESCENT BEHAVIORS

This section includes 5 reproducible newsletters for parents concerning various behaviors of preadolescents and adolescents featuring the following topics:

Dating or Associating with Undesirable Friends
Depression
Dieting
Dress and Grooming
Drinking and Drug Abuse

From:

DATING OR ASSOCIATING WITH UNDESIRABLE FRIENDS
Control, rather than forbid, the relationship.

When parents forbid something, they increase its appeal. The best way to deal with a child's dating an objectionable person or hanging around with undesirable friends is not to try to stop it, but rather to try to control how it occurs.

INVITE YOUR CHILD'S FRIEND TO YOUR HOME

If your teen is associating with questionable company, your best approach is to begin to invite the person or persons to your home. In fact, try to have them around as much as possible. This frequently allows your child to see them in quite a different light, and he/she may soon become disillusioned and end the relationship.

Consider the 16-year-old girl dating a 21-year-old unemployed man who was making no effort to find work. The girl's parents desperately wanted her to realize that the man was, in their words, "nothing more than a bum." Almost against their better judgment, they decided to invite him to dinner and spend some family time with him. Three weeks later their daughter said she didn't think her boyfriend was ever going to amount to much of anything. The parents did not respond to her remark. Four weeks later, the daughter announced that she had broken up with him adding, "I pity the girl who gets involved with him."

FORBID WITH CAUTION

When parents attempt to forbid children 16 or older from seeing someone, they should realize that unless they can keep their child under guard, he/she will find a way to see the other person. When parents attempt to control something over which they really have no control, they merely force their child to become deceptive.

Even if the parent's objection to a certain boyfriend or girlfriend can be enforced, there is residual ill feeling between the parent and the teen. Consequently, the price of winning can sometimes be quite high.

TROUBLE: POTENTIAL AND REAL

If a teen has been in trouble with someone and the relationship has no redeeming value, then parents might need to order the child to stay away from the other person. Before you can make that statement, make sure you can really enforce it. If the situation has the potential of causing trouble, it is best *not* to try to dissuade your child by pointing out potential dangers. Doing so will usually result in a stronger bond between the teenager and the undesirable person. Young people are not very likely to agree that something they want really is not worth the risk.

DIVERSION

Try to eliminate association with undesirable persons by attempting to involve your teen in other activities or by inviting desirable youngsters to participate in family events. As a last resort, you might have your teen spend the summer with someone who lives quite a distance away. If you go this route, do your best to make the time enjoyable for your teenager.

REMEMBER...

✔ Avoid forbidding your teen from seeing the other person.
✔ If you must forbid any contact, be sure you can control the situation.
✔ Provide other contacts.

From: _____

DEPRESSION

Learn to recognize the symptoms of depression.

When children feel unhappy or sad, they lose interest in activities they usually enjoy. When that happens, parents should consider the possibility that the child is depressed. Other common symptoms of depression are: complaining a lot about stomachaches, headaches, or other physical ailments; avoiding school and friends; and changes in sleeping habits such as sleeping too little or wanting to sleep all of the time.

Depression often involves a loss of appetite, but occasionally a child suffering from depression will overeat. Another sign of depression that is often unrecognized, except by professionals, is the tendency to develop behavior problems and to act out. This acting-out characteristic is very common with depressed teenagers.

In addition to the symptoms mentioned above, depressed teenagers frequently are attracted to the use of alcohol and drugs, seem insecure about their sexuality and about dealing with the opposite sex, tend to be semi-loners and not to have any close friends with whom they can talk, and tend to think that everybody else is much happier than they are.

DEPRESSION AND SELF-CONCEPT

In most cases, depressed individuals also have poor self-concepts. Parents must be careful not to say and/or do things to make the poor self-concept even worse. This generally happens when the child isn't performing up to his/her ability. Parents feel that their child isn't putting forth enough effort, so they begin to fuss at the child. This merely pushes the child into a deeper depression.

Parents must make every effort to help their children feel comfortable, good, and accepted. This helps to build the child's self-concept. With a strong positive self-concept, children can usually cope with typical situations without any major problems. Strengthening the child's self-concept is good advice for parents whether their child is depressed or not.

EVALUATION

Teenagers (age 13-19) who become depressed should be evaluated just like adults. This evaluation may include a recommendation for medication since depression may result from a chemical imbalance. Younger children may not need medication. Parents must not assume that their child will grow out of the depression and should usually have the child evaluated by a child specialist qualified to determine if depression exists and is severe enough to require treatment.

REMEMBER...

✔ Be alert to changes in your child's attitude and behavior.
✔ Look for changes in your child's sleeping patterns.
✔ Obtain professional help for your child.

© 1998 MAR+CO PRODUCTS, INC.

From: _____

DIETING

Train your child to eat the right foods, not to diet.

Some children are grossly overweight, but dieting in the sense of restricting how much is eaten and allowing the person to be hungry is not an advisable approach to weight loss for children or adults. Society has adopted dieting as a result of erroneously assuming that if food makes us gain weight, eating less should enable us to lose weight. Research, however, tells us that diets seldom work.

Repeated studies have shown that approximately 98% of all people who lose weight by dieting eventually gain it back and usually add a few extra pounds each time. Consequently, the long-range result of dieting is actually weight gain. This holds true for children as well as for adults. If the child learns appropriate eating habits, the weight will generally take care of itself.

On the other end of the weight spectrum, teenagers may have unrealistic concepts about slimness. In an attempt to reach this so-called "ideal weight," they may develop anorexia (severely limiting their intake of food) or bulimia (regurgitating food so the body does not absorb calories). Professional help should be sought for both conditions.

EAT THE PROPER FOODS

The key to weight control is eating the proper kinds of foods while avoiding the kinds of foods that complicate weight control. This means being careful with foods that contain fat. High-fat foods include all red meats (no matter how lean they look), oil, and pastries. Sugar should also be avoided. A person who wants to control his/her weight should eat his/her fill of fruits, salads, grains, vegetables, and fish. A food expert can provide advice about what and how much to eat.

EXERCISE

Another thing necessary for weight control is a regular exercise program that includes at least 30 minutes a day of walking, swimming, bicycling, aerobics, or some other form of cardiovascular exercise.

WATER

Teenagers and adults should drink at least 64 ounces (eight 8-ounce glasses) of water every day.

DON'T CALL ATTENTION TO WEIGHT

Avoid introducing your child to a program of dieting and focusing on dieting as a way of controlling weight. This frequently leads to excessive weight gain and eating disorders. Children should be taught that the range of normal weight is fairly wide.

One of the worst things parents can do is tell a child that he/she is getting fat and needs to lose weight. This has a reverse effect on children, and will actually foster behavior that will eventually result in weight gain.

REMEMBER...

- ✔ Avoid conveying the idea that you think the child is fat.
- ✔ Build exercise into the child's schedule.
- ✔ Prepare healthy foods. Teach your child to avoid "junk" foods.

From:

DRESS AND GROOMING

Avoid conflicts over grooming and makeup.

When teens over-use makeup, do not practice personal hygiene, or dress in an unacceptable fashion, parents should calmly state their concerns. If things do not change within a week parents should calmly say, "I love you very much, and that's why I feel I have to say something you may not want to hear. I hope you can see that your (makeup, dress, or grooming) is unacceptable, so I am asking you to change. This is the last time I ever want to talk about this. You have good judgment, and I am confident that you will realize that I am only asking you to do this because I love you and want what's best for you."

REFUSAL TO COMPLY

If there is no improvement after this second talk, parents should realize the child is not going to listen. If the issue is makeup or grooming, drop it. Continuing to press the point merely triggers rebellion. Remember that once your son or daughter is out of your sight, he/she can do as he/she pleases and even change clothes before returning home. This means you really have no control over the situation, and you are engaging in an exercise in futility. If the issue is indecent dress, simply get rid of the clothing of which you disapprove.

REMEMBER YOUR OWN TEENAGE YEARS

Did your parents ever object to your dress or grooming? If you are like most of us, you probably feel that you turned out pretty well in spite of that. You might be inclined to say, "But that was different." Was it really? Most children learn to conform as they mature. Remember that styles change. Putting pressure on your children to conform to your own taste is more likely to make the problem worse and cause a strained relationship between you and your child.

CONCENTRATE ON THE IMPORTANT ISSUES

Most teens don't dress in a sloppy or sexy fashion that, although unattractive to parents, is actually indecent. Yet some parents even go so far as to say, "You look like a hooker." Comments like this will not improve the child's appearance. *Never* call your child a name, because children have a tendency to live up to your expectations of them.

Other issues in parent-child relationships (such as maturity, responsibility, and love) are much more important than dress and grooming. Those things should not be sacrificed merely to get your child to dress in what you consider to be an appropriate fashion.

If you are finding it difficult to cope with your child's appearance, try to take a long-range view. Just because a child dresses sloppily or inappropriately now, doesn't mean this will continue throughout his/her life.

REMEMBER...

✔ Styles of dress change and children are inclined to conform as they mature.
✔ Don't use high pressure tactics; approach this topic from a position of love and concern.
✔ Do not call your child a negative name.

From:

DRINKING AND DRUG ABUSE

Most substance abuse takes place in social situations and a teen's social situation is often a party or small gathering of peers.

One of a parent's worst fears is drugs and alcohol. Even though a parent may use alcohol, they are fearful when their teen begins to drink. Will they drink too much? Will they drink and drive? Will they be in an accident? Will they mix alcohol and drugs? Will this become a habit they can not break?

SET GUIDELINES

No matter how much they protest, teens need guidelines and you should be open about what you expect. Guidelines are different than threats. Guidelines are what you expect, threats are what you will do if the guidelines are not met. Guidelines may include behaviors expected, limits, and curfew time. They should also include the fact that the children will be held accountable for their own behavior.

Threats can be dangerous especially if you are unable to carry them out. Many times, parents make such threats as, "Keep up this behavior and we are going to put you in an institution," when doing so may not be possible. Or, "If I ever catch you doing that again, you are out of the house forever," when you are probably not going to go that far.

If your child comes home sick as a result of drinking, don't pity or punish. The natural consequence of too much alcohol is punishment in itself. When the effects of the substance abuse have worn off, then discuss the occurrence and what both of you believe should be done. Don't cover for your teen by giving excuses or getting him/her out of school because of sickness caused by drinking.

DETERMINING IF A PROBLEM EXISTS

Ask yourself if substance abuse is interfering in any way with your child's ability to function. If the answer is "yes," a problem exists. If the answer is "no," remember because a person is functioning now is not a guarantee for future functioning and drinking under age or using drugs is still a crime punishable by law. Contact your child's counselor in order to learn how to deal with your child's substance abuse without making the problem worse. The Alcoholics Anonymous subgroup AL-ANON is another available resource.

FOCUS ON OTHER BEHAVIORS

If your child is getting up late for school, not getting chores done, or not doing well in school, focus on these behaviors instead of the alcohol and drug use that is causing them.

REMEMBER...

✔ Seek help if you suspect a problem.
✔ Avoid making threats.
✔ Focus on the behaviors caused by your child's alcohol and drug use.

PARENT BEHAVIORS

This section includes 17 reproducible newsletters for parents containing suggestions for positive parental behaviors featuring the following topics:

Apologies
Bluffing
Bribes
Coaxing
Developing Internal Motivation
Diffusing Anger
Distracting Children
Eavesdropping
Encouragement
Feelings of Inferiority
Giving Children Power
Leaving Children in the Care of Another Person
Parents' Screaming
Single-Parent Dating
Special-Needs Children
Teasing
Time Out

From: _____

APOLOGIES

Insist on improvement, not apologies.

Parents tend to place a high value on an apology. It is as if apologizing had some magical ability to change what has happened. In reality, apologizing won't necessarily improve a child's behavior. In many cases, apologizing is merely a license for children to repeat the same inappropriate behavior.

COMBINE APOLOGIES WITH IMPROVEMENT

Apologizing for inappropriate behavior is considered mannerly. But an apology is meaningless if it is not combined with a change in the behavior that made the apology necessary in the first place.

Parents must take steps to actually change the behavior involved. They need to sit down with the child and calmly work out a plan to help the child change. In the process, parents should ask the child what he/she thinks would work. Getting the child's input ensures greater success, since everyone works harder to make his/her own ideas work than to make someone else's ideas work. Remember, the purpose of the process is to have the child choose to change his/her behavior, not to force an apology. Parents can force a child to apologize, but not without resentment. When a child feels resentment, parents should be prepared for a reappearance of the inappropriate behavior.

When parents feel an apology is warranted, they can help children understand the importance of apologizing by asking how the child felt after someone hurt his/her feelings. Continue by asking if an apology would have made the child feel better about the person. Then point out that apologizing works both ways. By setting the stage in this way, you ensure that your child's answer to, "Do you think you ought to consider an apology?" will be the one you feel is correct.

FORCING APOLOGIES

Forcing a child to apologize usually makes him/her feel more resentment toward the person to whom the child is apologizing and is likely to result in more aggressive acts against that person. In order for apologies to work, the child must believe an apology is warranted. Children understand this concept when they realize that their behavior was inappropriate and they have a plan for eliminating such behavior in the future.

REMEMBER...

✔ Forced apologies cause resentment.
✔ Insist on appropriate behavior.
✔ Help the child understand how he/she would feel if the situation were reversed.

From: _____

BLUFFING

Bluffing is a dangerous game.

"If you don't behave, I'm going to put on my coat and leave this house."

Parents who use bluffing with children are skating on thin ice. The big question that parents who bluff must answer is, "What will I do if my child calls my bluff?"

BLUFFING AND COOPERATION

Many parents bluff in order to encourage children to cooperate. They threaten to do something they know they are not going to do. After such bluffs are used a few times, the child also knows the parent is not going to follow through. So, what have children learned? First, they have learned that paying attention to what parents say is not important. Second, they have learned that parents lie. When children believe parents lie, it is easy for them to rationalize that it is all right for them to lie, too.

BLUFFING SEEMS TO WORK

When parents begin bluffing, the strategy sometimes seems to work. Because of this, parents mistakenly believe that this technique will work with their children. Bluffing *can* work initially, but only for a short time, and it can lead to larger problems. Sooner or later, children are going to test the bluff. If parents do not follow through with what they say, children learn to discount what they hear. Over time, this tends to lead to a complete loss of respect for the parent, loss of the parent's authority, and a child who is out of control. Bluffing has taught the child that he/she does not have to listen to his/her parents (or, perhaps, to any authority figure).

CARRY OUT YOUR BLUFF

A *bluff* is another name for *threat,* and parents must ask themselves if they can live with the threat they have made and are willing and able to carry it out. If they are not, they should refrain from bluffing. For example, if leaving a child home alone is something a parent is not willing to do, the possibility should never be mentioned. The key words are *willing* and *able* to implement the statement. When parents threaten to do something when a child behaves in an particular way, the threat must be imposed if the child carries out the action. Parents must show that they are in charge and that they mean what they say.

REMEMBER...

✔ Bluffing is dangerous.
✔ If you say you are going to do something, you must do it.
✔ You must be *willing* and *able* to carry out any threat you make.

From: _____

BRIBES
Bribery can backfire.

"I will give you this ice cream cone, but you have to promise not to hit your brother again."

Saying something like this is like hiring a plumber to do a job and paying for the work in advance. Experience tells us that paying in advance is risky, as the worker may or may not do the job to our satisfaction. If the job has been paid for, and we are unhappy with it, we have no recourse. Paying in advance eliminates all control over having it performed satisfactorily. Receiving payment in advance also often eliminates the motivation to do a good job. This is true with children, too. First comes the performance, then comes the recognition.

CHILDREN OFTEN PROPOSE BRIBES

"Let me go to Susie's, and I promise I will clean up my room as soon as I get home." This is like the plumber saying, "Pay me now, and I will get the job done in a hurry." Would you be willing to take that risk? If not, then why accept the same type of proposal from your child? Not only are you taking a chance that the room will not get cleaned, you are teaching your child unrealistic practices for dealing with the real world. No employer is going to pay for work before it is performed and no teacher is going to give a grade before all the student's papers and tests have been completed. Follow the rule: First comes the performance, then comes the recognition.

Use the following statement: After you have (NAME THE TASK), then you can (THE RECOGNITION). For example, After you have picked up your toys, then you can go watch TV. After you have completed your homework, then you can go out.

BRIBES ENCOURAGE UNDESIRABLE BEHAVIOR

A bribe (as used here) is given *before* the task or behavior is performed. When a parent uses bribes, the child might do the desirable behavior at the moment, but at the same time learns what can be done to get another bribe (pay off) in the future. Therefore, the child has learned that acting out might result in a pay off. He/She thinks, "The last time I was hitting my brother, I got an ice cream cone."

A reward is only given *after* the desirable behavior (no hitting) occurs and avoids the problems associated with bribes. When using rewards, give them as soon as possible. Always include verbal praise along with any tangible reward. For example, when you are giving your child the ice cream cone (after the hitting has stopped), say, "You are learning to act grown up. You must be proud of yourself."

REMEMBER...
✔ Payment in advance for work involves risk.
✔ Use the statement: After you have _____ , then you can _____ .
✔ Bribes can encourage undesirable behavior.

From: _____

COAXING

Coaxing encourages resistance.

Coaxing is an attempt to persuade or strongly encourage someone to behave in a certain way. The more parents coax, the less likely it is that children will perform in the desired way.

COAXING GIVES ATTENTION

When parents coax, they are giving children a great deal of attention for *not* doing something. They coax and coax, and wonder why their children are still resisting them. The answer is easy—the children are getting attention for *not* performing. When parents realize this, it is easy for them to understand why coaxing backfires.

COAXING PROMOTES RESISTANCE

Every Sunday 13-year-old Mark and his family went to visit relatives. One day, without intending to, Mark found himself refusing to go. Nearly everyone in the family begged Mark to come along, but still he refused. Finally, they stopped coaxing and left him home alone. At this point, Mark felt miserable because he realized that he really would rather have gone along with the others. Mark could not explain why he had refused to go. In fact, as he sat home alone, Sunday after Sunday, he told himself that the next time he would go. But, each Sunday, he found himself repeating his resistive stance.

Many children, including teenagers, would quite readily agree to do something if it were not for their parents coaxing them. In many instances, the children actually *do* want to behave in an appropriate manner. When parents begin to coax, however, the children become more stubborn. They may not be aware of this, but they are subconsciously thrown into a position where they refuse to do something that they might otherwise have done. Many children have resisted to a point where a parent has given up, frequently with the result that the children become angry with themselves for having resisted so well.

It would seem that this would teach children not to be stubborn in the future. On the contrary, coaxing seems to *increase* the likelihood that the same resistive behavior will occur in the future.

DISCARD COAXING

If it does not matter whether your child does something, give him/her the choice. Since it does not matter, you can live easily with whichever choice he/she makes. If the child *must* do something, simply say so. The matter is then closed.

REMEMBER...

✔ Coaxing usually makes children more resistant.
✔ If the matter is not significant, give the child a choice and live with that choice.
✔ If the matter needs to be handled a certain way, tell the child how to do it.

From:

DEVELOPING INTERNAL MOTIVATION

Internal motivation is the key to responsible behavior.

Internal motivation means that a child behaves in a responsible way because he/she knows that is the right thing for both him/herself and society. A lofty goal? Perhaps, but one that can be fostered by supportive parenting.

Before children can perform a task properly, they need to be shown what to do. Too often, parents tell a child to do something without teaching him/her how to do it or not providing enough training. They may say to themselves that they showed the child how to do the task three or four times already and that the child should know what to do. This is not always the case. Irresponsible behavior is likely to occur when a child is asked to do something he/she hasn't been adequately trained to do. When training a child to do something new, encourage him/her by saying something like, "You are learning this very quickly," or "You must be proud of yourself for the good job you are doing."

Children like and seek out those things that make them feel good. If children who have never cleaned their rooms are suddenly expected to do so because they have reached a certain age, a parent who expects a perfect job is unrealistic. However, the parent who understands that learning new tasks takes time and recognizes the improvement each time the room is cleaned, is the parent who is establishing patterns of behavior that will lead to accomplishment. It is important to recognize improvement even if it is not yet adequate. Too often parents withhold recognition until the job is perfect. This does not encourage the child to persevere.

Also, do not criticize the performance or the part that is not "up to par." Criticism seldom serves as a positive motivator. It usually elicits undesirable behavior.

Parents who notice their children doing something well and make statements like, "How proud you must be of yourself for doing such a good job," help their children associate feeling good with acting properly. These good feelings far outweigh any of the external rewards parents often feel are necessary to encourage children to act properly or perform a task correctly. There is more to be gained from saying, "You must be proud of yourself for accomplishing _____ ," than from saying, "You did a good job." While the two statements may appear to be saying the same thing, the first statement not only encourages like the second one, but, by identifying the accomplishment and including how the child feels, helps to internalize motivation.

REWARDS

If you use tangible rewards or verbal praise, use them in conjunction with the statement, "You must be proud of yourself for (MENTION THE ACCOMPLISHMENT)." When you later withdraw the reward, your child will tend to continue to be motivated by the internal feeling of satisfaction.

REMEMBER...

✔ Criticism seldom motivates.
✔ Identify your child's accomplishment by saying, "You must be proud of yourself for (MENTION THE ACCOMPLISHMENT)."
✔ Don't overlook even the slightest improvement in your child's behavior.

From:

DIFFUSING ANGER

When arguments occur, respond in an agreeable fashion. Then raise a question.

Arguments can cause great family stress. Whether they occur between children and parents, siblings, or children and friends, they are times that no family looks forward to and problems that families want to resolve as quickly as possible.

ARGUING BREEDS ARGUING

When there is a disagreement between you and your child, arguing about it is futile. Arguing only leads to more discontent and anger. Each party feels that he/she is right and each party wants to win. Since nobody wins as long as the arguing continues, it is important to find ways to stop the arguing and settle the conflict.

UNDERSTAND AND QUESTION

You can often diffuse anger by finding some way to sound as if you understand the problem. A statement like, "I agree that it seems unfair to you," often works. This statement does not say that you agree with the child's opinion, only that you understand why he/she feels your decision is unjust.

A second statement that raises a question is designed to make the child think. For example, "I agree that this seems unfair to you. What do you think we can do about it?" promotes *thinking,* rather than lashing out. The use of the word *we* signals the child that you are going to help him/her find a solution. Use these statements exactly as they appear here unless you are sure you have a better choice of words.

STOP THE ARGUMENT BEFORE IT BEGINS

Of course, it is better to avoid getting into an argument in the first place. To do this, you must remember several things. Never argue with a child over something you want him/her to do. Arguing about a task or behavior encourages the child to rationalize and defend his/her behavior. Simply tell the child what is to be done. If he/she chooses not to comply, apply a consequence. Parents who know they are in charge do not show displeasure. They feel secure in the requests they make and don't worry if their directions are not followed.

A proverb says, "He who becomes angry first has already lost the argument." Quote this to your children when they are old enough to understand its meaning.

REMAIN CALM

When children approach you in an angry fashion, remain calm. If the child is angry at another person, listen but do not try to solve the problem. If the child is angry at you, say, "When you calm down and are ready to talk about this sensibly, I am ready to discuss it." If the child is unable to calm down, ignore the behavior by walking away or going back to what you were doing. Do not continue to talk to the child. Say nothing more.

REMEMBER...

✔ Never argue with a child over something you want him/her to do.
✔ Tell the child what to do. If the child does not follow your instructions, apply consequences.
✔ Diffuse anger by showing the child that you understand how he/she feels.

From:

DISTRACTING CHILDREN

Distracting children from inappropriate behaviors can help cement parent/child relationships.

Chris and Michael both like the same video game. Fighting over who gets to play with it is common in their home.

Tiffany has recently taken up with a group of teenagers who have been in trouble at school.

When parents rely on saying *no* to behaviors they dislike, they often make the behaviors more appealing. Young children soon realize that continuing the objectionable behavior draws more and more attention to them. Older children resent and rebel against the authoritative approach.

Distraction is one way to effectively deal with disturbing behaviors. When children are fascinated with breakable objects, parents can draw their attention to something more interesting and less fragile. The same technique can be used when two children are fighting over a toy. Another way of dealing with fighting children is to put the toy away so that neither child can play with it. This technique can also be used to redirect teenagers. Encourage them to become involved in sports, get a job, or become interested in a hobby that will take up their time. If a child is too busy to associate with undesirable friends, the problem might solve itself.

REDIRECTING

In most situations, it is easier to redirect a child's attention than it is to deal with the fuss that results from saying *no*. The parent whose child does not challenge or question his/her authority is very fortunate. Most children *do* challenge parents and try to persuade them to say *yes*. Redirecting a child's attention helps prevent this fuss.

TIME-OUT BREAK

When children are fussing with each other, announce that it is time to take a break. This could involve giving the children something to eat, playing a game, going to the store, or doing anything that will distract the children from the fussing. After the break, the atmosphere will usually improve.

AVOIDING CONFLICT BUILDS RELATIONSHIPS

Whenever parents say *no*, they risk becoming part of a conflict. This results in a less-than-satisfactory relationship, since no one is very quick to comply with a request or demand made by someone with whom he/she is in conflict. Use *no* sparingly, and only when you cannot think of anything else to say or do. Instead, explain why the child's behavior is inappropriate, apply a consequence, or redirect his/her interest. The more successfully parents maintain a positive relationship with their children, the more likely they are to receive their child's cooperation.

REMEMBER...

✔ Use *no* only when you cannot think of anything else to say.
✔ When children are fussing with each other, announce that it's time for a time-out break.
✔ Use redirecting or distracting techniques to refocus the child's attention.

From:

EAVESDROPPING

It is incredible how strongly eavesdropping can influence a child's behavior.

Eavesdropping, as used here, is when parents have a discussion about the child in such a way that the child can overhear a conversation he/she *thinks* was supposed to be private.

THE SETUP

Have the conversation in a private place, such as your bedroom. Leave the door slightly open and choose a time when the child is certain to overhear what you are saying. The conversation consists of both parents alternating between expressing doubts and beliefs that the child is capable of behaving or not behaving in a certain way. It might go something like this:

Father: I used to think Jimmy was really grown up. I used to think he was capable of cleaning up after himself, but now I'm beginning to have some doubts about that.
Mother: I know what you mean. I've begun to have some doubts about whether Jimmy is grown-up enough to know how to clean up his room. You know, the other day I did see him straightening his room, though.
Father: Well, maybe you are right. I saw him clean up the mess in the kitchen, and I didn't have to ask him to do so. You know, when he does these things I believe he is really responsible, and then we have a day like yesterday when he didn't clean up the mess in the living room.
Mother: I remember that too, so maybe he isn't that responsible after all. I would like to think he is, but it certainly isn't a clear picture. As I'm talking, I remember that there was a lot of clutter in the corner of the dining room yesterday and he cleaned it up without even being asked. That's when I am so impressed with him and really believe he is growing up and becoming mature.
Father: It certainly doesn't seem very clear whether he is mature enough to clean up. I guess we'll just have to wait and see.
Mother: I guess you're right. We'll just have to see over the next few weeks whether he is responsible enough to do these things.

After a discussion like this, wait a few days and look for changes in your child's behavior. If no improvement occurs within a week, have another similar discussion and be certain that the child hears the performance. If the child wants to prove he is capable and mature, he will work very hard at improving.

USE THIS TECHNIQUE FOR MANY BEHAVIORS

This technique can be used with children who have problems getting up on time, cleaning up messy rooms, getting to school on time, getting along with children, and a multitude of other behaviors.

The main point to keep in mind when using this technique is to emphasize maturity and capability. Make it sound as if the issue is a question of skill and maturity.

REMEMBER...

✔ Children really listen when they think they are overhearing something they are not supposed to hear.
✔ Practice this technique before you "perform" for your child.
✔ The "eavesdropping technique" can be used for many issues.

© 1998 MAR+CO PRODUCTS, INC.

From:

ENCOURAGEMENT

Criticism often discourages children from trying.

Many times, parents try to get their children to behave in a certain way by pointing out what the children are not doing properly or by criticizing them.

"Because you didn't pick up your clothes, your room looks like a garbage dump."

"Will you ever learn that you are supposed to do your homework right after school?"

Unfortunately, this common tactic does not work. Psychological research has repeatedly shown that only a small percentage of children actually improve their behavior as a result of this type of interaction.

Encouraging children is a better approach. This means finding whatever good there is in a situation and mentioning only that. This may seem impossible when the child's bedroom is an embarrassing sight and his/her grades are falling because homework isn't being turned in on time. However, recognition of good qualities motivates children to try harder. This, in turn, enables them to improve.

EXPECTING TOO MUCH TOO SOON

It is important not to expect too much from your child. If you do, you might not provide the encouragement that your child needs to improve his/her performance. Remember that you can break any skill into small segments and work at accomplishing each small part until your child learns the desired behavior. Begin by expecting the child to either make his/her bed or pick up his/her clothes. When the first task has been accomplished, add another. It is important to encourage children by giving them tasks that they can perform. If parents expect too much, it stops development.

SHAPING

Shaping is a technique used by animal trainers. The same type of procedure, on a higher level, works well with children.

An animal trainer who wants to teach a dog to dance on its hind legs might wait until the dog lifts its body weight off its front legs. Then, even if the dog isn't actually dancing, it is rewarded with a treat. This process continues until the dog learns to keep its front paws in the air. Sooner or later, the dog will be dancing.

It takes a little more skill and ability to know how to successfully apply behavior shaping principles to children. If a parent wants a child to do homework immediately after school, then he/she must pay attention every time the child comes home, sits down, and gets the work done. In order to motivate the child to complete all his/her homework, parents can ask the child to show them what has been accomplished after 10 minutes of work, then lengthen the time span to 15 minutes, and so forth until the child is able to complete the task without interruption.

REMEMBER...

✔ Criticism discourages performance.
✔ Encouragement fosters performance.
✔ Shaping is an excellent way to foster skill development.

From: _____

FEELINGS OF INFERIORITY

*Play up your child's good points.
Play down unsuccessful areas.*

Criticism doesn't motivate many children. Name-calling teaches children to live up to the expectations of the name. Negative nicknames have the same effect.

Unfortunately, many parents believe the way to get children to do better is to criticize their poor performance. This belief is often rooted in the fact that the parents themselves were reared with criticism. Since this is what they know best, this is the approach they use. This very risky approach should be abandoned in favor of one of the well-founded and reliable approaches described below.

NOTHING BUILDS SUCCESS LIKE SUCCESS

Children who are encouraged and who experience success will build on their experiences and enjoy even more success. It is important to be wary of how *success* is judged. Many children judge their own success by the way others perceive them. In other words, if children are truly successful, but believe their parents do not see them in the same way, they will not view themselves as successful persons.

The best way to help a child build a positive self-concept and avoid feelings of inferiority is through large doses of positive strokes. No matter how poor a child's performance is, there are some things that he/she is doing correctly and properly. To best help children develop their skills, concentrate on whatever they do well.

Shyness causes some children to avoid trying to learn new things. Parents must be careful not to let their children avoid life because that, too, will lead to increased feelings of inferiority. These children can be fearful of life and cling to parents when faced with situations that make them uncertain. Pressing children too hard is also dangerous. Continually pushing children to do better, without recognizing what they have already accomplished, can cause them to feel that they will never be good enough. The wise parent knows when and how hard to encourage children without applying too much pressure and without allowing children to escape the realities of life.

ENVIRONMENT IS THE KEY

Most children absorb feelings of security or insecurity from their environment. Personality and hereditary factors are an influence, but most feelings of inferiority can be traced to environmental experiences. This is why it is so important that a child be given a good, positive, and healthy environment in which to grow and develop a sense of positive self-worth. Unfortunately, our society tends to put people down rather than build them up. With a positive self-concept as their cornerstone, children can almost always be successful in whatever realm or vocation they pursue.

REMEMBER...

✔ Criticism usually discourages children. It seldom motivates them.
✔ Success builds success.
✔ Find and recognize what is good or improved.

From:

GIVING CHILDREN POWER

Putting children in charge can change their behaviors.

A child who is never on time can be put in charge of watching the clock and making sure other family members are punctual.

A child who never completes chores can be put in charge of the chore chart, supervising chores to be done by everyone in the family, and making sure each chore is recorded on the chart.

Parents can often solve behavior problems by placing a child in charge of supervising the area in which he/she is most negligent. Most parents don't think of doing this. Instead, they are inclined to pick the child who performs the task the best to be the supervisor. The reasoning behind this technique is that when a child is put in charge of a behavior that he/she does not do well, the child becomes so involved in making sure everything is done correctly, that energies are diverted away from ordinarily disruptive behavior.

RESPONSIBILITY BREEDS RESPONSIBLE BEHAVIOR

It is not unusual for a child who has been put in charge of something to experience an almost immediate behavior change as a result of the new responsibility. However, children are not all alike. They must feel a sense of responsibility in order for this technique to be successful. You may have a child with whom the technique will not work quickly. You may feel the approach is not successful because your child did not respond the first time or two you tried it. Be sure to give the child several opportunities before discarding the technique. If, after a trial period, the technique really isn't successful, discontinue it. You have lost nothing by trying it.

If a child litters, put him/her in charge of keeping the house or lawn tidy. If a child doesn't pick up things, put him/her in charge of seeing that everything is picked up. The list of ways this technique can be applied is almost endless.

RESPONSIBILITIES OF BEING IN CHARGE

Being in charge does not mean sitting back and bossing everyone else around. It *does* mean having control over getting things done properly. For example, the child who is messy could be put in charge of seeing that things are picked up in the house. The child must not only pick up his/her own things, but see that other family members do not leave their things laying around. This is power based on responsibility to yourself and to the task that needs to be done.

REMEMBER...

✔ Put the negligent child in charge of the problem area.
✔ Being in charge does not mean being bossy.
✔ Being in charge builds a sense of responsibility.

From:

LEAVING CHILDREN IN THE CARE OF ANOTHER PERSON

Begin leaving children with competent baby-sitters at an early age.

Sometimes a child throws a tantrum to try to prevent parents from leaving him/her with friends, relatives, or baby-sitters. Guilt-ridden, the parents change their plans and stay home. To avoid a similar scene, many parents do not even attempt to leave again at a later date.

LEAVE AS SCHEDULED

The best way to handle this type of situation is to leave as planned. When parents change their plans to accommodate a tantruming child they reinforce his/her fear of being left in the care of others. This can eventually cause the child to become insecure.

Making an issue of a parent's departure through long discussions that describe the parent's plans to leave and attempting to assure the child that he/she will be safe and happy and the parent will return, only reinforces children's fears and insecurities. Parents should tell children who ask where they are going and approximately when they will return. This is often when children start trying to convince their parents not to leave. The mistake that most parents make at this point is to start talking with their children and attempting to persuade or convince them that everything will be all right. The more parents talk, the more fearful children become. It is best to make the statement once, then leave.

DON'T SUCCUMB TO CRYING

Some parents find it difficult to leave a crying child. If they give in to this crying, they are being hooked into a situation that is ultimately going to be detrimental to the child. When this happens, parents must leave, knowing that the child will be fine while they are away from home. Generally, after the parent leaves, the child stops crying and *is* fine. After children get used to their parents going out without them, they stop the fussing and crying.

BEGIN AT AN EARLY AGE

When a child is a few weeks old, parents can begin using a competent baby-sitter. Parents who never leave their children with another adult until the children are old enough to start school often find themselves meeting with the school psychologist or counselor. Their children are fearful of any separation, and school becomes a nightmare with children crying in the morning, parents trying to coerce them into the classroom, and other children wondering why *that* child is so different. Children who have successfully dealt with separation from parents are generally able to go to school without any fears or problems. The earlier children learn to deal with separation, the easier it is for them.

REMEMBER...

✔ Leave children with a reliable person early in their lives and continue to do so frequently.
✔ Never change your plans because a crying child doesn't want you to leave.
✔ Tell the child where you are going and when you will return. Then leave, and make every effort to return on time.

From: _____

PARENTS' SCREAMING

Screaming may cause your child's behavior to worsen.

We have all seen children respond negatively to adults who use screaming as a form of discipline. We have seen the same child act well-behaved around a calm adult.

WHY SCREAM?

Although almost everyone knows that screaming doesn't work, many parents continue to do it. Why? Maybe it has become a habit or maybe the parent screams because he/she feels insecure. If it is a habit, it can be changed. Parents who scream out of a sense of insecurity may need to seek counseling to learn some techniques that will enable them to remain calm when their children challenge their authority.

A person who feels in charge of a situation can remain calm. A person who is unsure, frightened, or does not feel in control tends to scream. It is important for parents to give children the impression that they are in control, even if they do not feel that way. If children sense that a parent is rattled, they can use the parent's insecurity to get their own way or the awareness may trigger insecure feelings in children that cause them to act out emotionally. Either way, parents are creating more hassles for themselves. Parents who can remain calm convey a sense of authority and a sense of being in control.

SPEAK IN A STRONG, FIRM VOICE

Using a strong, firm voice when disciplining children is the most effective way to get the message across. When parents scream, the child's behavior usually worsens. When children hear a high-pitched voice, they feel as if they are being scolded. This screaming or nagging often triggers a more intense desire to do the very thing for which they are being scolded. A firm, low-pitched voice, on the other hand, tends to get the listener's attention.

In order to speak in a firm and deep voice, you must be calm. When a parent is not calm, the volume and pitch of his/her voice usually rises. This means that parents tend to lose influence over their children when they become upset. Children seem to sense when parents are upset and vulnerable. When this happens, parents are at a distinct disadvantage when attempting to get children to change their behavior. Children know which buttons to push to get what they want and parents are easy prey. Staying calm is so important because a parent's stability and control provides the atmosphere for the child's stability and cooperation. Remember, parents who *know* they are in charge are not easily rattled.

REMEMBER...

✔ Avoid yelling and screaming.
✔ Be calm, or give the appearance of being calm.
✔ Speak in a controlled, calm, strong, firm voice.

From: _____

SINGLE-PARENT DATING
Children need stability.

Should single parents inform their children whenever they go on a date?

If a single parent does not tell children about the first date, when do they begin to involve the date and the children with each other?

With the number of divorced and single parents in today's world, the issue of dating and step-parenting is rather common. If this is an issue in your life, remember that children need stability. Consequently, if you bring too many new friends home as potential parents, your children derive a real sense of insecurity and instability. The rule of thumb here is: If it is just a casual date, inform your children that's all it is and don't try to get them and your date involved with each other. On the other hand, if you are becoming quite serious about the person you are dating, don't delay involving your children until the person is ready to move into your home.

THE SERIOUS DATE

If your relationship is becoming serious and your date is going to be very involved in your family, you and your children need to have a family discussion. Allow your children to express themselves about this matter, and don't be surprised if there is some opposition to it. Your children may feel that this new person is trying to replace the absent parent and adamantly resist that. Sometimes the opposition is based on fear of the unknown. Fear always accompanies change, and children perceive this as a reason to *oppose* rather that *accept* the new person.

Very few children want a new parent. Under no circumstances should you expect or try to force your children to love the new person. Respect, love, and admiration take time. If the person you are dating is truly a good person your children will eventually come around to accepting him/her. This will happen more quickly and easily if you do not start by trying to force acceptance.

Dates need guidance, too. The person you are dating should be reminded not to impose him/herself on your children as if he/she were a new parent. Statements like, "I'm going to be your new dad, and I expect you to do as I say," should be avoided. It is wise to state, "I know you miss your dad, and I'm not going to try to replace him. I hope that we can become friends." In the beginning, the new person should try to let the natural parent deal with major issues. It is important for him/her to be involved in the discussion, but the natural parent should set the rules. As time passes, he/she should assume a more authoritative role, not because he/she is the child's parent, but because he/she is an adult.

REMEMBER...

✔ Do not tell a child that you are his/her new father or mother.
✔ Let the child decide whether to call you *dad* or *mom*.
✔ Realize that any change in family structure is a frightening experience for a child.

© 1998 MAR+CO PRODUCTS, INC.

From:

SPECIAL-NEEDS CHILDREN

Don't do things for children that they are capable of doing for themselves.

Parents of special-needs children must be careful not to fall into traps that will make their children more dependent. Because of the child's special need, it is easy to feel sorry for his/her lot in life. Parents often think that special-needs children deserve special treatment because they have been "through so much." What these parents don't realize is that special treatment can cause the child to become more dependent and, consequently, suffer more, rather than less, pain in life. Compare this to the analogy of either giving the poor man a fish or teaching him to fish. If you give him the fish, then all you have done is helped him momentarily. In the future, he will go hungry unless you can always be there to feed him. On the other hand, if you teach him to fish, he can function on his own and won't ever have to go hungry again.

RECOGNITION HELPS DEVELOP NEW SKILLS

If there is some kind of special ability or skill the child needs to learn, recognize every improvement. This is the most advantageous way of helping the child develop a new skill, because it motivates the child to become more adept at performing the task. Waiting for the child to complete the entire task before recognizing his/her progress, almost guarantees that the task will never be completed.

When a task is broken down into steps and each step of accomplishment is recognized, children learn more quickly. For example, think about the child whose physical handicap makes writing very difficult. If the parent waits until the child writes his/her name properly before recognizing the progress, the child probably won't ever learn to write and will never receive any recognition. On the other hand, if the parent recognizes when the child learns to hold the pencil properly, and the child learns to make a mark resembling the first letter of his/her name, the child is more likely to learn to write.

MAKE A SPECIAL-NEEDS CHILD'S LIFE AS PRODUCTIVE AS POSSIBLE

Special-needs children can have a difficult time in life. Parents can help them learn skills that will ease their everyday living but, these children may need to be encouraged more than other children. However, the encouragement must reflect the child's ability level and rate of learning. Very severely handicapped children should not be pushed to do things they cannot learn to do. These children will need someone to care for them. Parents who are not sure how hard to push their child should consult a professional who knows the child.

The rule of thumb is: Encourage and assist special-needs children, but don't do for them what they are capable of doing independently. Overcome the temptation to further handicap these children.

REMEMBER...

✔ Recognize every improvement your child makes.
✔ Teach the skill. When the child has learned it, let him/her do it alone.
✔ Don't let feelings of sympathy further handicap the child.

From:

TEASING

Never tease children.
If your child is teasing others, take action.

Parents who continually tease children are very likely to cause problems for their children. Parents' comments are taken seriously by children, and it is possible for one comment to make a permanent impression. Sometimes parents think teasing a child will improve their behavior. It won't.

TEASING A CHILD

Teasing a child, or teasing anyone, can result in psychological barriers that make the individual feel so uncomfortable that he/she won't engage in certain behaviors. For example, if a child begins to play basketball and is made fun of or teased, he/she probably won't play the game again.

Teasing also undermines self-confidence which, in turn, results in several other problems. Children with poor self-concepts tend to be withdrawn, afraid to try new things, and generally do not do as well in school as their classmates. There is a tendency to foster the problem toward which the teasing is directed. In other words, teasing someone about being stupid is very likely to make him/her act in a stupid manner. There is no reason to take that chance. Your child is too important to risk. This is why teasing needs to be prevented or stopped.

In dealing with children, there is no such thing as "teasing for fun." Parents can use less-dangerous ways to have playful interaction with their children. Everyone likes compliments. Find something good to say to your child and avoid negative comments. Rather than tear down your child's self-concept, try to bolster it.

Remember, teasing is similar to name-calling. Most parents don't want to call their children names and don't want their children to call others names, so it stands to reason that they should not approve of teasing.

CHILDREN WHO TEASE OTHERS

If a child teases other children, this problem needs to be dealt with by taking away privileges, rather than "giving the child a dose of his/her own medicine." In other words, don't punish children by teasing them. Instead, take away TV, bike-riding, or playing with a particular child for a day. Punishment for teasing should be brief. As a general rule, it should be kept to one day at a time.

REMEMBER...

✔ Parents who tease may cause problems for their children.
✔ Build up your child's self-concept; don't tear it down.
✔ Do not allow your child to tease others.

From: _____

TIME-OUT

Time-out helps children change their behavior 99% of the time.

Sending children to a time-out place for a period of time is one of the most effective techniques parents can use. It works because it deprives attention and because it puts the child in a mildly uncomfortable situation from which he/she wants to escape. To escape uncomfortable situations, children are almost always willing to improve their behavior.

THE TIME-OUT ROOM

When children act inappropriately, they should be sent to a place that separates them from everyone else. The place should be well-lighted, not a dark place or a closet. If the room has a door, it may be closed, but do not lock it. This is a time to separate the child, but not have him/her become fearful of being locked up. The child's room is often not the best place for time-out because the child's toys are there and because you do not want the child to view his/her room as a place of punishment. Sometimes a bathroom works well, but parents who use the bathroom as a time-out zone need to be positive that it contains no sharp objects, medications, or anything else that might injure the child or be used to make a mess. A child who is being toilet trained should not be taught to associate the bathroom with punishment. Find the place that seems like the most suitable for a time-out zone in your home. Try it. If it does not work, look for another area.

Most children don't attempt to destroy property during time-out. They *do* often cry or kick the door. Crying should be ignored, so should kicking the door, as long as you can repaint or even replace the door later. If your child attempts to actually destroy things, additional steps must be taken. One is to strip the room to the point where there is nothing in it that can be destroyed. Although this may present an inconvenience for a short period of time, it is rarely necessary to live with this situation for more than a week or two. By that time, the behavior has usually been corrected and the room can be refurnished. When this is the case, the best choice for time-out is usually the child's room emptied of toys.

IGNORE EXCUSES

Excuses, such as having to go to the bathroom or needing a drink of water, should be ignored. Remember that when the child is in the time-out room, the child does not exist. Very few children will soil their clothes. If they do, put up with the problem until the behavior changes. When a child is in time-out there should be no communication between you. Nor should there be communication when the child is sent to time-out. The child should be taken by the arm and placed in the room, and the parent should say nothing. A child should remain in time-out for the number of minutes equal to twice his/her age. For example, a five-year-old child should be sent to time-out for 10 minutes. The timing starts when the tantruming ceases. If the child leaves time-out and repeats the misbehavior, start the procedure over again.

REMEMBER...

✔ Time-out is one of the best techniques for changing behavior.
✔ A child remains in time-out for the number of minutes equal to twice his/her age.
✔ Parents have no communication with the child during time-out.

ACADEMIC CONCERNS

This section includes three reproducible newsletters for parents concerning various school-related topics featuring the following topics:

Fear of School
Homework
Note-Home Program

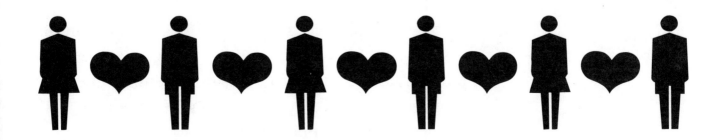

From:

FEAR OF SCHOOL

Show understanding, but send your child to school.

Many times the fear of going to school is really the fear of leaving the parent. If the parent is ill, the child may feel that staying home will prevent something bad from happening to mom or dad. Sometimes the fear of school is triggered by a parent saying, "I'll be so lonely without you here." The child feels that staying home will make the parent feel better. Sometimes the fear of school has to do with a specific teacher or an uncomfortable environment. If this is the case, listen to your child. Then explain that although you understand he/she must still go to school. Before bedtime, say, "In five minutes, it will be time to get ready for bed so you will be ready to go to school tomorrow." This helps the child realize that you expect him/her to go to school.

INVESTIGATE THE PROBLEM

If the problem at school can be identified, then it can be investigated. This may mean taking the child to school early or staying after school. It may mean spending some time alone with the child in the school environment. This can be a wise thing to do with children who are going to school for the first time or with children who have a history of school phobia. If the parent and child can make several visits to the school shortly before the school year starts, it helps the child to see school as a familiar place.

SPENDING TIME AT SCHOOL

A parent whose schedule includes some free time during school hours might check with his/her child's teacher to see if it permissible to sit in the classroom for part of a day. A parent who uses this technique should gradually spend less and less time in the classroom, until the child goes to school without fear. The parent might also sit in the car in a spot the child can see from the classroom window. The parent who uses this technique should gradually spend less and less time sitting outside school.

BE FIRM

If the preceding suggestions don't work, there is a more drastic approach which is almost always successful. Transport the child to school in a matter-of-fact way, deposit the child on the school premises, and drive away. Knowing that the child will be quite upset, make prior arrangements for one of his/her teachers to be available to comfort the child. This forges a bond between the child and the teacher which enables the child to feel comfortable at school.

The biggest problem parents face with this method is feeling that they are being cruel. Parents must realize that the child may not just stay home from school and that the parent cannot stay at school with the child for the next several years. Even though the child may be upset at first, the teacher will be there to provide comfort and, in a short time, the problem will be solved. In order for this technique to work effectively, parents must be able and willing to deal with their own fears and beliefs about their parenting skills.

REMEMBER...

✔ Be firm about the fact that the child *is* going to school.
✔ Visit the school before the school year or class begins to familiarize the child with the school environment.
✔ Treat this matter calmly. Do not show emotional distress for the child to play upon.

From: _____

HOMEWORK

Improve your child's homework skills by structuring his/her home-study environment.

The issue of homework brings to mind several common problems. Children forgetting to copy down, find out, or remember what the assignments are; forgetting to bring homework home; failing to do homework; and failing to turn in completed assignments are issues that turn homework into a nightmare for both parents and children. If these are issues you face, here are some ways you can deal more effectively with these concerns:

- Provide the child with a special notebook just for homework assignments. Nothing else is to be written in this notebook.
- When homework assignments are completed, the work is put into the special notebook so it can be turned in at school.
- Ask teachers to send a note home with the homework assignment which parents must sign and return.

SCHEDULING

It is best to have the child do his/her homework at the same time every day. Meals and bedtime are at regular times, and giving homework the same consideration gives it equal importance. The time will vary from household to household. A half hour after arriving home from school gives children time for a snack, but not time to get involved in other activities. If you feel playtime is essential after being in class for the day, then set a time for children to do their homework after they have had some time to play. The difficulty here is getting the child to stop playing and start working. Work should usually come before play, especially if the child is having difficulty remembering or completing assignments.

"I ALREADY DID MY HOMEWORK"

Sometimes children act as though they have already completed their homework when, in fact, they have not. When this happens, parents need to take a few additional steps. If the homework is something like math that can be checked, allow the child to go out to play only after the homework has been checked and approved. Reading is another matter. It is easy for children to pretend they have read an assignment. Check this by taking the child's reading material and glancing through it to find a few questions to ask him/her. Pick two or three easy questions that will let you quickly determine whether the child has read the material.

STUDY HABITS BEGIN AT AN EARLY AGE

Good study habits should begin in the first grade. Insist that no radio or television be playing while the child is doing homework. Studies have repeatedly shown that most people learn better in a quiet atmosphere. Be willing to help, but don't do your child's work. If you feel your child needs help, make up a new problem similar to the homework problem, show him/her how to do it, and then have the child solve the original problem on his/her own.

REMEMBER...

✔ Use a homework notebook.
✔ Set a regular time for doing homework.
✔ Check and approve homework before the child goes out to play.

© 1998 MAR+CO PRODUCTS, INC.

From: _____

NOTE-HOME PROGRAM

Bringing a note home each day from the teacher can improve a child's academic work and behavior.

The *Note-Home Program* can be used to improve either behavior or academic performance, but should be used only when other techniques have failed and if the teacher agrees to participate. It is a program that requires parents to be very consistent in their own behaviors.

GRADE RATING

The note the teacher sends home should contain: the child's name, the date, and a letter grade (A to F) for the child's overall performance for that day. If the child has had a problem with homework, a statement should also be included about the child's homework for that evening. The teacher should initial the note.

If the behavior targeted involves academic work, the grade given is an average for all the work done in the course of the day. If the child does very well in the morning and very poorly in the afternoon, an overall grade of "C" may be appropriate. The grade should not be based on a particular subject or test.

If the child's primary problem has to do with behavior, then the grade is based on the child's behavior throughout the day for the targeted behavior. If the child's problems are both academic and behavioral, it is generally better to correct the more significant problem before addressing the other one.

PARENTS' RESPONSIBILITY

Once the note arrives home, the parent uses the following formula for determining what privileges the child has for that evening. These decisions should reflect each household's particular situation. An example could be: An "A" merits all the TV and play time the child desires from the time his/her homework and chores are finished until it is time to get ready for bed; a "B" merits 90 minutes of TV and play time; a "C" merits 60 minutes of TV and play time; a "D" merits 30 minutes of TV and play time; an "F" merits no TV, no play time, no privileges at all. If the note does not arrive at home, privileges are to be restricted as if the child had received an "F." This prevents the child from losing the note or forgetting to bring the note home.

Parents must have patience. It may take up to two weeks for the program to start working. It is important for parents to be consistent and persistent.

REMEMBER...

✔ When school performance and behavior determine privileges at home, the child generally improves quickly.

✔ Don't fall for statements such as: "The teacher forgot," and "I lost it."

✔ To make this program work, both parents and teachers must be very consistent.

HOUSEHOLD CONCERNS

This section includes 11 reproducible newsletters for parents concerning various issues that arise in the home featuring the following topics:

- Allowances
- Bedtime
- Children of Divorce
- Chores
- Getting Up on Time
- Going to the Hospital
- Music Practice
- New Baby in the Family
- Room Cleaning
- Visiting the Doctor
- Working Parents

From: _____

ALLOWANCES

An allowance is a tool for teaching life skills.

Many times, parents are uncertain about whether it is appropriate to give children allowances. There are two theories about allowances. One theory ties an allowance to completing chores and another theory ties it to learning to handle money.

ALLOWANCES AND CHORES

Some people believe tieing an allowance to specific chores or duties helps children develop a sense of responsibility. They also believe that giving children money without expecting something in return is training children to expect handouts from life. If using this method, be wary of teaching children to expect payment for every thing they do around the house. Explain that certain tasks are expected of them because all members of a family contribute to the good of the family team. When a child asked to do an additional chore asks, "How much will you give me if I do it?" it is a signal the parent has fallen into the allowance trap.

LEARNING TO HANDLE MONEY

This theory suggests providing children with a certain amount of money each week and requiring them to be responsible for certain expenses. These expenses might be an extra toy, a special event the child would like to attend, clothing in addition to what parents have bought, etc. Although this type of allowance is not directly tied to chores, chores are not eliminated from the child's existence. The difference is that chores are expected and required because the child is a member of the family. If they are not completed, a consequence other than withholding money is applied.

Parents who use this theory believe that children need to learn to handle money efficiently. This is especially true in a society, like ours, that provides easy-to-get credit cards and experiences frequent bankruptcies.

EXTRA MONEY FOR EXTRA CHORES

Children often want to earn money for one purpose or another. This can be beneficial for both the child and the parents. One way to handle this is to have a list of extra jobs children can do around the house. Specify the fee to be paid for each job. When a child asks if there is anything he/she can do to earn extra money, show him/her the list and decide together which job would be best for the child to do.

WHEN TO BEGIN GIVING ALLOWANCES

Giving allowances can begin at an early age. In fact, the earlier the better. Parents should be reasonable about the amount of the child's allowance. The amount should be based on common sense and on what the family can afford, not on what the neighbors are giving their children. If the family is financially well off, parents must be careful not to give the child too much money. Begin with a smaller amount and raise the allowance as the child gets older.

REMEMBER...

✔ Choose the allowance method that best fits your family's beliefs and goals.
✔ The most common allowance error is parents being too generous.
✔ Learning to handle money responsibly is an essential life skill.

From:

BEDTIME
Avoid bedtime traps.

Children often act out when it's time for them to go to bed. They do it to get attention, not because there is anything wrong. They learn that by crying or making frequent requests to go to the bathroom, they can involve their parents in a conversation and avoid doing what they don't want to do.

INFANTS

Infants have a tendency to cry when being put down to sleep. If this happens with your child, check with a physician to make sure there is nothing physically wrong. If nothing *is* wrong, take the following steps. When the child begins to cry, check to see if there is a physical problem. If there is no problem, leave the room and do not return unless the child continues to cry for more than 5 minutes. At this point, go in and quickly recheck the child physically. If the child is fine, pat him/her on the back a few times and leave. This should take about 20-25 seconds. If the child continues to cry, the parent should remain out of the room for 10 minutes before going back in to check on the child. This procedure should be followed until the child is asleep. In other words, the first check takes place after 5 minutes, but subsequent checks on the child should be made at 10-minute intervals.

TODDLERS

A slightly different approach is recommended for toddlers. First, it is important to establish a regular and definite bedtime routine. After a child has been very active, it is often virtually impossible to get him/her to calm down enough to feel sleepy. The parent should create a time for the child to wind down before going to bed. For example, the child can be told that in 5 minutes it will be time to get ready for bed. After the child is in bed, the parent may talk to the child for a few minutes or read a story for no more than 5 minutes. After that, it is time for the parent to leave the child's room.

YOUNG CHILDREN

If a child who is more than three years old begins to cry, ask what is wrong. If the child can't give an adequate explanation, refrain from going into his/her room until at least 10 minutes have passed. At that point, enter the room, pat the child on the back a few times, and leave. Do not return unless the child is still crying after another 10 minutes. If the child is still crying, repeat the same procedure.

OLDER CHILDREN

If an older child has a tendency to get the parent involved by saying, "I have to go to the bathroom," "I want a drink," etc., the parent must pretend that he/she didn't hear the request. If the child comes out of his/her room, the parent should quickly, without saying anything, take the child by the arm and escort him/her back to the room, put him/her in bed, and leave. The key is not to say anything during the process. Sometimes children's requests are legitimate. Parents have to be sensitive to legitimate requests and careful to recognize requests that are traps to get them involved.

REMEMBER...

✔ Establish a routine.
✔ Once the child is in bed, avoid getting involved.
✔ Do not allow yourself to become engaged in conversations that are attempts to avoid going to bed.

From: _____

CHILDREN OF DIVORCE

Make every effort to make your divorce as painless as possible for your children.

Children handle divorce most successfully when parents work together for the sake of the child they both love. In most cases, children are emotionally bonded to both parents. These bonds are very important. Parents should not try, either consciously or unconsciously, to destroy them. If the other parent destroys the bond by his/her behavior, that is not your fault.

BE POSITIVE

Divorce is not a pleasant situation. It almost always results in bad feelings. Parents are as emotionally wounded as their children. Because the children are the ones most closely connected to the ex-spouse, it is easy to vent negative feelings against the other parent to them. Parents who have a tendency to say negative things to their children often lose out in the long run.

Sometimes this behavior is a conscious or unconscious attempt to turn the child against the other parent. However, attempts like this merely cause the child to defend that parent. Keep in mind that it is "my dad" or "my mom" that you are talking about. While you may manage to alienate the child from the other parent at first, such tactics almost always backfire. As children get older, the resentment they feel often turns onto the parent who has made the negative remarks. Don't risk your relationship with your child in this way. If you cannot say anything good about the other parent, don't say anything.

If the other parent makes negative remarks about you, keep your cool. Do not retaliate. If the allegation is specific, do not get overly involved in trying to explain or justify it. It is often best to simply say, "You know me. Do you believe I would do anything like that?" Too much justifying is perceived as attempting to cover something up. The less you say, the better.

Children need a sense of security and roots. If a parent is going to say anything about his/her ex-spouse, it should be positive. Remember, it is the child who is important and not the hurt or angry feelings of the parent. It is important not to lie to the child, but it is usually not necessary to bring up sordid material. Parents can always refuse to talk about private issues even if the child asks about them.

If you really love your child, you will not play him/her against your ex-spouse. You will let the child sort out his/her own feelings about the other parent.

PUT YOUR CHILD'S WELFARE FIRST

Ideally, you and your ex-spouse will work together in the best interest of your child, who needs both of you. *Working together* means never trying to keep a child from his/her parent unless neglect or abuse is involved. It means not asking, "Do you love me more than you love your dad? (or mom?)" Never say anything that might be repeated to your ex-spouse.

REMEMBER...

✔ Do not make negative remarks about your ex-spouse.
✔ Do not use your child as a pawn in your battles with your ex-spouse.
✔ Your child's happiness involves having a relationship with each of his/her parents.

From: _____

CHORES

Introduce responsibilities at an early age and increase them gradually.

One mistake parents frequently make when assigning chores is to assign too many chores all at once. Another mistake is making the chores too big or demanding. When this happens, children perceive the task as overwhelming and they don't even attempt to accomplish what they have been asked to do.

Chores for children should begin with things like having a toddler pick up his/her toys. Young children (four to five years old) often want to help. Take advantage of this natural desire and give the child a chore to do. It is important not to assign anything that will burden the child. When the task is completed, recognize and praise the child. This type of reaction usually results in the child wanting to do more things to please you. Start with one chore, and do not add another until the first chore is being done properly. Add chores slowly, building from simple ones to those that are more complex. When involving the child in family chores, it is important to instill the idea that everyone in the family has chores. Dad cuts the grass. Mom washes the clothes. Your brother empties the trash, and you clear the table after dinner. Children need to realize that chores are a part of family life and a cooperative effort.

SELECTION OF CHORES

Parents can help children choose chores. Parents can make up a list of suitable chores for children to do, discuss them with the children, add any acceptable ones the children think should be included, and decide together who will do what for the next week. After assigning the chores, post a chart and tell the children to check off each chore as it is completed. The chart eliminates parents having to remind their children to do what they have already agreed to do. If parents get into the habit of reminding children, children are less likely to do their chores on their own. Completed chores can be recognized by playing a special game, visiting a friend, choosing the evening meal, etc. Incomplete chores can result in such consequences as not being allowed to play until chores are finished, loosing a privilege, etc.

WHEN CHILDREN REBEL

The issue of chores often becomes the focus of a child's rebellion. Children may refuse to do chores or refuse to do them properly as a way of attempting to exert their own authority while a parent, at the same time, is attempting to prove that he/she is boss. Conflict results. Unless parents are willing to stand over their children to see if they are performing their chores, the forceful approach is unlikely to work and will cause problems for the family. Wise parents know how to motivate their children and do not have to stand over them. The key, then, is to discover what will prompt the child to do what is expected, and if agreeable to you, use it as a motivational technique.

REMEMBER...

✔ Start assigning chores early.
✔ Add chores gradually.
✔ Instill the idea that chores are a cooperative family effort.

© 1998 MAR+CO PRODUCTS, INC.

From: _____

GETTING UP ON TIME

Children should be responsible for getting themselves out of bed on time.

In many cases, parents' attempts to get their children up in the morning merely encourage them to stay in bed. Here are some tips to help you overcome this problem and teach your children responsibility.

CHALLENGE

Challenge children with a statement such as, "I'll bet I can get ready for work before you can get dressed for school." This type of challenge is almost always met with enthusiasm by a child. Be sure the child wins, and make a fuss over his/her accomplishment. Discontinue the technique after a few months. By this time, the behavior will probably be well-established and the child will continue it on his/her own.

GET AN ALARM CLOCK

If a child fails to get up in time, a parent will often awaken the child and keep nagging him/her to get out of bed and keep moving. Buy an alarm clock and teach the child to use it. Almost all children of school age can shut off the alarm set by a parent the night before.

Some children will not get up at the sound of the alarm. They lie in bed expecting and hoping the parent will get involved. Resist this temptation, even if the child will be late. If the child gets up too late to catch the bus or his/her ride to school, avoid encouraging or urging the child to hurry. Comments about being slow give the child desired attention. If the child walks to school, then he/she leaves the house whenever he/she is ready and accepts the consequences of being late to school. If the child misses the bus or his/her ride to school, the parent should take the child to school at his/her convenience or make the child stay home. If you take the child to school, inform the school office why the child is late. If you keep the child home from school, be sure the day is spent doing schoolwork. It is important that staying home is less enjoyable than going to school.

If allowing the child to be late for school also makes the parent late for work, then the parent must make sure the child gets to school on time. In this case, have the child "pay back" the time that was spent urging the him/her to get ready. That evening have the child go to bed the amount of time "owed" earlier than usual.

TAKE STEPS THE PREVIOUS NIGHT

There are things a parent can do at night to increase the likelihood that a child gets up the next morning. At bedtime simply say, "It is time to go to bed now so that you will be able to get up tomorrow morning when the alarm rings." This lets your child know what you expect.

REMEMBER...

✔ Buy an alarm clock and expect the child to get up on his/her own when it rings.
✔ Avoid saying, "Hurry up, you'll be late."
✔ If the child is late getting to school, be sure the school is aware of the reason.

From:

GOING TO THE HOSPITAL

Tell children that being in the hospital will help them get well.

Be as honest as you can about a hospital stay. Explain why the child is going to the hospital, what will happen there, and if there is going to be any pain. But always be sure to add that the hospital will help the child get well.

YOUNG CHILDREN

Children who are very young will often derive security from having some of their possessions with them in the hospital. If the child has a favorite toy or blanket, check with the hospital to see if he/she may bring that item. Very few hospitals will object. Permit the child to take, within reason, whatever he/she wants as long as it is acceptable to the hospital.

PARENTAL INFLUENCE

Parents have a tremendous influence on how quickly their children recover from serious illnesses or surgeries. Having something to look forward to can greatly encourage children to get well. A child who has nothing to look forward to but going home and putting up with hassles from brothers and sisters or hearing parents fight is going to have a delayed recovery. On the other hand, children who expect to take a special trip or go to a fun place are motivated to get well quickly. Tell the child about something specific that is going to happen when he/she gets well. Mention it often, especially when you leave at the end of visiting hours. This will give the child something positive to dwell on and will help pass the time.

VISITING HOURS

Most hospital pediatric sections have flexible visiting hours. Parents can often plan to stay with a hospitalized child 24 hours a day if they wish. In general, it is best to spend no more time there than the child seems to need.

HOSPITAL BILLS

Be careful not to discuss doctor and hospital bills in the child's presence. Children are aware enough to know if these bills are a problem for the family and could see themselves as a burden or expense. If the child asks about the bills, it is best to say, "Yes, there is going to be some cost, but we love you and will take care of it. You just get well."

GIVE REASSURANCE

Being in a hospital can be frightening. Anxiety delays healing, and makes the time spent in the hospital more unpleasant. Tell the child about someone he/she knows who was in the hospital and is now home and well. If the child is in pain, recall an incident when he/she went from having pain to having no pain in a short time. If you say, "It does not hurt," to a child, the child will have to show you how much it *does*. Instead say, "I know it hurts, but it will get better in a short time."

REMEMBER...

✔ Remind the child that the hospital is a place to help him/her get well.
✔ Plan something fun for the child to look forward to after the hospital stay.
✔ Give reassurance without dwelling on the negative aspects of being sick and in the hospital.

© 1998 MAR+CO PRODUCTS, INC.

From:

MUSIC PRACTICE

Concentrate on how the child's performance is improving rather than on the time he/she spends practicing.

All of us know how to spend time on a task without accomplishing much. Children, too, can put in many hours of practice and still not learn much. To encourage accomplishment in a sport or music, concentrate on how hard the child is working, not on the amount of time spent practicing. Focus on what the child learns. If the learning takes place in half an hour, allow the child to stop.

LEARNING—NOT AMOUNT OF TIME

Most parents and instructors emphasize that improvement depends on practice. Unfortunately, they often emphasize how long they want children to practice. While that makes logical sense, it doesn't, in most cases, motivate children to practice efficiently. Most children will be more motivated to learn if simply asked to learn the material or a skill by a certain time and no practice time is stipulated.

TIMING FOR PRACTICE IS IMPORTANT

Schedule practice at a time in which the child gets lots of attention or recognition. Doing this will help instill good feelings about and pleasant associations with practicing. One motivator would be to offer a favorite food after a good practice session. This will increase the motivation to practice correctly in the future. Use caution when looking for motivators, and do not use the same one every time. Doing so will cause the child to lose interest. Notice children while they are practicing or after they have finished practicing. Give the child a hug and say a positive comment like, "I am really proud of how much you have learned in such a short time." Simple gestures like these are extremely rewarding and motivating for a child.

HOW TO HELP

To help your child learn an entire lesson, break the material into sections and tell the child that each section is to be learned by a certain time. Then, insist that each part of the lesson be completed before the practice session ends. If a child wastes time and takes two or three hours to learn a specified part of the lesson, he/she quickly learns that the harder he/she works, the more quickly free time becomes available. This type of built-in motivator encourages children to work at their peak and learn skills in a fraction of the time that otherwise might be required.

REMEMBER...

✔ Performance is what is important, not the amount of time spent in practice.
✔ Break the lesson into parts.
✔ Children may waste time, if they choose, but they must stay with the assigned task until it is completed.

From:

NEW BABY IN THE FAMILY
Older children need to be helpers.

When parents don't make special attempts to get their older children involved in taking care of a new child, they run the risk of having the older children feeling that the attention they had formerly received now belongs to the new arrival. This occurs no matter how many older siblings the new baby has. If it is the second child, the first child had never had to compete for attention. If there is more than one older child, they had less siblings with whom to compete.

GAIN OLDER CHILDREN'S COOPERATION

The best thing a parent can do is to involve older children in the anticipated arrival of the new baby and solicit their older child's cooperation in helping care for the new infant. Include older children in shopping for things for the new baby, selecting a name, and preparing the room. If the older children are mature enough, show them how to bathe, dress, feed, and diaper a new baby. Practice with a doll before the actual arrival. Explain how much care the new baby will need. In short, provide the older children with as much information as possible before the baby comes home. Making them feel a part of the process will make older children feel included, rather than excluded.

RECOGNIZE HELP AND APPROPRIATE BEHAVIOR

When the baby arrives home and the actual care begins, noticing and praising older children for their attentiveness and cooperation can produce several advantages. The older children have no need to act out to get attention. They are getting attention for appropriate behavior. The older children are forming a good association with their new sibling. The parents' relationship with the older children is positive, rather than negative. Don't keep your older children's good works to yourself. Tell friends, relatives, and neighbors, in the presence of the older children, about their helpfulness.

RESENTING THE NEW BABY

Sometimes older children feel resentful toward their new sibling. In some rare cases, they have even tried to hurt or harm the infant. If your child's attitude seems resentful, you may express disappointment, but don't panic and react against the older child and show protective emotions toward the infant. This merely increases the likelihood of further resentment of the infant. Rather, say, "You are my special helper, and we need to take good care of the baby. Will you help me do that?" Keep your voice calm, even though you are anything but calm inside. If the resentment persists or if the child could cause potential harm to the infant, seek counseling.

REMEMBER...

- ✔ Involve children in preparations for the new arrival.
- ✔ Enlist older children to be special helpers.
- ✔ All children need attention, and a new baby makes competition for parents' attention more intense.

© 1998 MAR*CO PRODUCTS, INC.

From:

ROOM CLEANING
Give recognition for improved performance.

Children's failure to keep their rooms clean is the basis for many a family argument. Parents who want to include room cleaning as part of a child's household duties should begin the training process at the age of five or six. Divide room cleaning into several tasks, concentrating on one until the child does it well. Then focus on a second task, and continue until the whole job is accomplished.

BE SPECIFIC

Parents need to be specific about what exactly constitutes a clean room. If necessary, make a checklist, post the list in the child's room, and check off each task as it is performed. Always recognize improvement. Even if a bed is not made exactly to your standards, if it looks better than it did the day before, tell the child that you have seen improvement. Recognition motivates children to continue to do better.

BE CONSISTENT

Many parents excuse children from chores because they are doing something they enjoy. For example, if a child wants to play the guitar, but was told to clean up his/her room first, the parent may hear guitar music coming from the bedroom. At this point, the parent may let the child get by without cleaning the room because he/she does not want to discourage the child from practicing the guitar. This is when the parent must realize that there is no reason why the child cannot practice the guitar and still be neat. If this type of situation needs to be addressed, parents should not criticize the guitar playing, but merely point out, without mentioning the guitar, that the room is to be cleaned.

SET SPECIFIC TIMES

Another area in which the cleanliness of a child's room becomes a point of discussion is time. Parents frequently want the child to clean the room immediately. This can result in conflict. It is generally wiser for the parent to give the child some time to do the job. Specify this time and do not keep reminding the child of what he/she must do. If the job does not get done, impose some restriction.

IT'S MY TURF

With older children, the issue of room cleaning becomes one of *turf*. It is further complicated by the issue of self-direction. Many teenagers would choose to be neat, but if parents say they must clean their rooms, they become stubbornly rebellious. Teenage rebellion is an attempt by the older child to establish an identity as an independent person who makes his/her own decisions. Sometimes it is wise to tell the child that the way the room is kept is his/her choice. The hope is that, after a while, the child will choose to clean the room. This can work if the child has his/her own room, and the parent can "live with" whatever the room looks like until the child decides to clean.

REMEMBER...

✔ Room cleaning begins at an early age by assigning age-appropriate tasks.
✔ Set specific times for room cleaning.
✔ If room cleaning is a hassle, decide whether a clean room or your parent-child relationship is more important.

From:

VISITING THE DOCTOR
Be as truthful as possible about the impending visit.

Visits to the doctor can be frightening to children if parents do not take the time to prepare them. Explain why children need checkups. Explain why a child who is ill must go to the doctor. If you know that the procedure the doctor needs to do might cause some pain, tell the child, "The doctor may have to hurt you a little, but what the doctor is going to do will help make you well." Do not think you are saving children from grief by misleading them. Be truthful. If you are not, you break down their confidence and trust in you.

DON'T AVOID VISITING THE DOCTOR

Parents must do what is in the best interest of their children. Sometimes parents refrain from taking a child to the doctor because the child refuses to go or because the parents don't want the child to go through some medical procedure that might make him/her uncomfortable or inflict pain. Remember, sometimes you have to allow some pain to be inflicted in order to prevent something more painful from happening.

Do not argue with children about whether they should go to the doctor. If you have determined that medical services are needed, inform the child, explain your reasons, and go to the doctor. If the child tries to argue and talk you out of it, refuse to become involved. State what is going to happen and do not discuss it further.

If the child continues to complain and argue, treat the behavior like any other annoying behavior. Ignore it. Every parent has a breaking point. Parents who reach the breaking point often act in ways that are generally unwise. Catching yourself before you get to that point can result in a thoughtful and effective action. One action would be to remove yourself from the presence of the child. When you are no longer together, complaining has no purpose.

FEARFULNESS

It is understandable that a child who has undergone a painful medical procedure in the past may be apprehensive about revisiting the doctor. Under these circumstances, anxiety arises very quickly in children. When you notice this happening, calmly state, "Yes, there are times when the doctor must hurt you, but it is not what the doctor wants to do. The doctor just wants to help you get well." It is important to say this in a non-emotional fashion. If you come across as being very emotional, the child will become even more upset.

REMEMBER...

✔ Be truthful about the visit to the doctor, but add, "It will help you get well."
✔ Don't argue with a child about going to the doctor. Do what needs to be done.
✔ Speak in a non-emotional tone of voice when discussing a doctor's visit with a child.

© 1998 MAR•CO PRODUCTS, INC.

From: _____

WORKING PARENTS
Provide your children with the safest possible environment.

Ideally, a parent should be home with children at least until they begin school and, preferably, until the age of 12. But that is not practical in most families. Our society is based on two incomes instead of one. A parent who must work outside the home should not feel guilty about leaving his/her children in the care of one or more responsible adults.

SPECIAL TIME

When both parents work, it is critical that each one take some special time to be with their children. Each parent should plan to spend at least five minutes each day with each child, giving the child the parents' complete attention. This is the time to listen and talk about the day or about some plans you have to do something together.

DAYCARE

If your child will be in daycare, check out the facility. Ask for permission to come and spend at least three hours observing the class your child will attend. Wait around outside and talk with at least three parents about the program. Call the local Department of Human Resources or its equivalent and ask if any complaints have been filed against the center. Your children are your most valuable possessions, and you should never feel pressured to put them in a place with which you are not comfortable. Teach your child about good touching and bad touching.

TEACH SAFETY RULES

Children under the age of 13 should have supervision after school. In some cases, children older than 13 may need supervision.

If children must be in an unsupervised situation, discuss a special telephone signal and teach your child not to answer the phone unless he/she hears the signal. One signal could be to ring the phone twice, then hang up and call right back. Your child should never go to the door unless he/she definitely knows who is there. Even if someone claims there is an emergency, the child should not open the door for anyone he/she does not know well. Teach your child to call 911 or the local emergency number for someone in distress.

Do not allow your children to have friends in your home when no adult is present. Instead, have them do their homework, so that when you are home, they will be free to visit or invite friends to visit.

REMEMBER...

✔ Spend special time with each child every day.
✔ If daycare is necessary, carefully check out the facility before enrolling your child.
✔ Teach your child safety rules and procedures.

ABOUT THE AUTHORS

Robert Kline has a background in the ministry and in child development. After obtaining a Masters of Divinity, he earned his doctorate from Brigham Young University. He was a member of the faculty at Auburn University for a short time, then entered the mental-health field. After serving nine years as Clinical Director of the four-county Regional Mental Health Center in rural Alabama, he entered full-time private practice. He was recruited by the Alabama Institute for Deaf and Blind, and has been a psychologist there for the past 10 years while maintaining his private practice. Over his 24 years of professional service, he has evaluated, counseled, and worked with thousands of children and their families.

Julie E. Kline is the daughter of Robert and Marilyn Kline. She is a third-year doctoral student at the Georgia School of Professional Psychology.